M000112591

Rock Ur World

A Life and Leadership Handbook for College-Bound Students

Bridget Markwood

Chili Pepper Press

ISBN: 0989848507
ISBN-13: 978-0-9898485-0-3

This book is dedicated to all of the students
with whom I've had the pleasure to work–
past, present and future.

CONTENTS

Acknowledgments   i

You as a Leader   2

Characteristics of a Leader   18

Effective Communication   30

College 101   42

Getting Involved on Campus   60

Leading a Team   76

All About Events   88

In the End   106

INTRODUCTION AND ACKNOWLEDGMENTS

"Look. Listen. Choose. Act"
Barbara Hall, Television Producer

For the last 15 years, I have been working with students, just like you, on leadership development. One thing I have learned is that listening to you is the most important factor in my helping with your development. For several years I gave students the same information everyone else does, in a similar way. Then, I realized that some of the information assumed that students knew things they had no way of knowing and some of the information was baby food for this generation.

To help with this, I sat down with numerous groups of students, ages 15-22, and asked them a lot of questions. What do you want to know about leadership? What do you not want to hear about anymore? What are some of your greatest struggles? What do you find confusing about leadership, about college, about life?

This book is based on those responses. It is about your journey. Whether you become a great president, the CEO of a company, the neighborhood "mom," or choose to do something else entirely different, leading is about influence, more so than position. You can influence someone in a variety of ways. Knowing how to lead a team also helps you to be a better team member.

There is nothing in this book that will hurt you to know. It can only make you stronger and wiser. Even if every section doesn't apply to you yet, it may at some point... so this is a good book to keep on your shelf after you have read it.

Sprinkled throughout are sections called Unique 2U. These are sections about Millennial (that's your generation) issues. They are issues that no other generation has had to deal with. Mostly, they involve technology and its use in leadership.

I give a special thanks to those who lent their assistance and advice as to the content of this book: Christopher Markwood, Ph.D., Melissa Koberlein, Ph.D., Brooke Wilson, M.Ed., MeShawn Conley, M.Ed., and Kyle Johnson. And I am so very grateful to Catherine Quick, Ph.D. who lent her time, energy, and professional skills to get this book ready for you.

Enjoy the book, enjoy the quotes, and please, enjoy your wonderful life!

Bridget

YOU AS A LEADER

This first chapter is all about YOU. The person you are, the decisions you make and your perception of people and the world around you will determine the type of leader you are or will be. Think about the concepts in this chapter and how they apply to you today. Know that you will change over the next several years. Referring back to these sections will help you in your discovery of yourself and hopefully help to keep you strong through the hard times.

> "Leadership development is a life-time journey- not a brief trip."
> John Maxwell, Author

Self Assessment

Before you can begin to develop your leadership skills, you first must take a look inside of yourself. It all starts with you. There are so many issues students must wade through each day, that figuring out who you are and where you stand can be quite complicated. In this section, we explore the self. Many ideas posed in this chapter may hit close to home- and that can be uncomfortable. But I encourage you to think about them honestly. This is for your growth.

Self-Worth

Self-worth is just what it sounds like- how *valuable* you think you are. Those with a higher self-worth are those who usually take the initiative to go out there and do great things with their lives. They feel that they are an important part of this world and know that they have something to offer. Those with a low self-worth are generally going to shrink into the background, not feeling as though they have a contribution to make.

Working with countless students over the years has proven to me that every student, every human being, has something to offer (yes, including you). You have strengths that a team is lacking. You have a way of looking at something that others do not have the benefit of without you. You are priceless.

Think about it...It was not until the dawn of the motion picture that people could become famous for doing nothing really important. For millennia, those we looked up to had to truly accomplish something with their lives- help others, invent something useful, get elected- before the masses of people looked up to them.

Actors, actresses and models, though they work hard at their jobs, really do not have to do anything special with their lives in order to be famous. They do not even need to have any sort of moral code by which to live. If you really want someone famous to look up to, choose someone who has done something for a cause you believe in. Pick a true hero to be your role model -famous or not.

"Nothing so conclusively proves a man's ability to lead others as to what he does from day to day to lead himself."
Thomas J. Watson (1874-1956), Former President of IBM

Self-Concept

Your self-concept is what you *think* about yourself. There are two major areas of self-concept we will be exploring, physical and psychological.

Physical Self-Concept- How you see yourself

One aspect of your physical self-concept is what you think of yourself, physically. How do you like the way you look? Do you like your hair, your body shape, your face? Are you healthy? This is a difficult area for most students. We are told we should have flatter tummies, bigger muscles, longer/shorter hair, certain piercings, etc.

The big problem with all of this is that we tend to think that having all of these things will change who we are and our concept of ourselves. It doesn't. There is always going to be something else "they" say we should have. Getting caught up in "what they say" is getting stuck playing a game that never ends. No winners there. Exercising, eating right, resting, playing (in other words, living a physically balanced life) will make you feel better, but that's because being healthy makes you feel good.

Physical Self-Concept- How you think others see you

Another area of your physical self-concept is how you think others view you physically. Often, we get these two areas confused. We think that others think we are too fat or are not pretty, so we begin to believe it.

> *Leaders are unique individuals, not perfect ones.*

Here is the truth. If you accept you, others will accept you. No one really notices a not-so-perfect detail unless you make it the focus. If you don't like something about yourself, change it. If you can't change it, embrace it. If you are aiming to be like everyone else, you are aiming to be a follower. Set your standards higher than that; love who you are. Don't believe me? Try it out on someone you've never met. Just have a conversation with someone and act like whatever "flaws" you think you have aren't an issue. It will surprise you how unimportant that issue is to others. They will take their cues from you.

Psychological Self-Concept- How smart you think you are

This affects what you are willing to take on. If you do not think you have the brainpower to handle something, you are probably not going to chance it. Please know that most everyone can handle more than they think they can. Another thing to remember is that there are different types of intellect. The astrophysicist may not be smarter than the philosopher, they are just different types of people, who think and process information differently. One of the neatest things about humans is that we are all so different. If everyone was good at the hard sciences (biology, chemistry, etc.), we would have no art, no song, no novels, etc.

Psychological Self-Concept- What you think/feel about your interests

This is how we view our hobbies, areas of special study, things we collect, what we like to do on the weekends, etc. It is so easy to fall into the trap of, "well, everybody else likes it, so should I." The truth is, you should do what you like. If you want to do something that the others are not doing, start a new fad or a new organization. Lead. You never know, all of those others may not want to be doing what they are doing; they may just be waiting for something better to come along.

Self-Esteem

Your self-esteem is how good you *feel* about yourself. Feelings imply emotions. Emotions are fickle. Take a moment and think about how many emotions you feel in one day. Someone triggers anger, someone else happiness, something causes anxiety, something else causes you to relax, and on and on... Because esteem is based on emotions and emotions are relevant to what is going on at any particular moment, our esteem rises and falls based on what is going on in our lives. If someone tells you that you are the best thing since sliced bread, you are probably going to feel pretty good about yourself. However, if someone tells you

> The _key_ to keeping positive self-esteem is to understand that you have a _choice_ whether or not to accept anyone's opinion of you.

that you did something really wrong, you might feel bad about yourself.

Sure, we all make mistakes. We should learn from them, grow from them, and then move beyond them. You are more than a product of any given action. You are more than any amount of actions. You are the fabulous person inside.

Self-Confidence

Self-confidence is how you *project* yourself. The way you project yourself directly affects the way others perceive you. If you are confident, others will have confidence in you. If you are not sure about yourself, others will not be sure about you either. Now, there is a difference between being confident and being cocky. Cockiness says that you are closed to what others think and feel. Confidence says that it is okay for others to add to the conversation, project, etc.

People want to follow a confident leader. So how do you get there? By exploring the areas of the self we have already discussed. By deciding you have a high self-worth and you are valuable. By examining your self-concepts, changing what you can (if you do not like it) and accepting/ celebrating the things you cannot change. By finding ways to feel good about yourself, you increase your self-esteem.

> *Never be afraid to admit you do not know something or to ask for help.*

Even the strongest leaders do not necessarily feel super confident the first time they try to tackle something. Your first time leading a project, you will probably feel a little uneasy about it. After all, you do not want to make a mistake or lead others in a wrong direction. However, people will not feel comfortable with your decisions unless you are sure of them. The advice here is to be open to the suggestions of others, make a decision, and be confident in it. You are a leader, not a loner.

> "Have confidence that if you have done a little thing well,
> you can do a bigger thing well too."
> David Storey, English Playwright, novelist and former athlete

The Enemies of Your Self

After examining the positive areas of self, it is easy to feel good about yourself. You might be saying, "I can do that; I can see that. Dang, I feel pretty good about myself now." Well, if you are…fantastic. There are, however, a few other items that need to be addressed. We all know that life is not perfect. In fact, several times a day (at least) we allow the enemies of our selves to invade. Looking at these enemies head-on will help you to combat them when they do creep in.

Self-Doubt

Oh, yeah. The arch-enemy of self-confidence. "I'm not strong enough; I don't know enough; I'm no good at ____; I shouldn't have said that; They think I'm stupid."

Oh my goodness!!!! Stop torturing yourself!!!

"You never conquer a mountain. Mountains can't be conquered; you conquer yourself- your hopes, your fears."
Jim Whittaker, (1st American to reach the summit of Mt. Everest)

No human being on the face of the earth is perfect (in that cookie-cutter perfect sense). We doubt ourselves when we do not feel we are living up to "perfection." Words to live by…Strive only to be *your* best *self*. Whatever that means to you. The key words being "your" and "self." You have talents, strengths, abilities, a certain body type, and certain features. You are unique. A cookie-cutter makes the same shaped cookies time after time after time. What about making your own cookie (so to speak) and molding it so it suits you?

Is self-doubt ever a good thing? Yes. Self-doubt can help you to not make bad decisions. When self-confidence starts turning in to cocky, all self-doubt is gone. That is not a good thing. Self-doubt in your decision-making can force you to look at multiple sides of an issue. That is a good thing.

Self-Pity

To tell you that life will always be great is a flat lie. Life has a way of handing you things that are hard to go through. You might lose someone close to you. You might lose a job or not get a job you really want. You might not, no matter how hard you try, get a grade you want. In life, you will probably disappoint someone you love at some point. You will probably make a really bad decision that you regret. You will probably not do everything you want to do. These are realities. They are not meant to depress you; they are meant to give you a heads-up. Life happens. Sometimes life is unbelievably great and other times it's incredibly difficult.

> "The marvelous richness of human experience would lose something of rewarding joy if there were no limitations to overcome. The hilltop hour would not be half so wonderful if there were no dark valleys to traverse."
> Helen Keller (1880-1968), Author, Lecturer, Political Activist

When life does get difficult, you have choices to make. First, understand that there is a natural process all people go through during hard times. You may feel angry, depressed, in denial, you may try to bargain. These are all normal. During these times we grow so much, often not realizing it until more time has passed. There will, however, come a point when accepting what has happened is necessary to move forward.

When one chooses not to move forward, one gets stuck. Self-pity is what happens when it is time to move ahead in our lives and we do not. We get stuck in thinking, "Why did this happen to me? If only I had… I wish I could just…" People have gotten stuck there for years, decades even. When you are stuck somewhere that means you are not going anywhere. You cannot move along in life or in growth until you are able to forgive whatever it is (including yourself). Your life is so short in the grand scheme of time. You have, at best, 100 years to live on this earth. You have only that time to do whatever you need to do to contribute to the world and your community. The longer one spends in self-pity, the less time one has to make a difference.

Again, please understand it is normal and healthy to grieve and/or to fully examine something after it happens. The key is not to get stuck there.

Self-Destructiveness

Too much time in self-doubt and/or self-pity will lead one to a self-destruct sequence that is very difficult to stop. Trying to find where we fit in this world is perhaps one of the most difficult tasks we face in our lifetimes. Students undertake this task every day. Fitting-in in high school, selecting a major in college, finding a true friend, or finding a true love (or not) can all make life very difficult for young adults today. Self-doubt and self-pity are so easy to fall back on.

There are many ways self-destructiveness shows its ugly face. Drugs and alcohol are big ones. Why do people use them? Students often find them easy replacements for self-confidence. Students who are shy (and feel that they should not be for some reason) feel less inhibited when they use. By the way, some people are just introverted (see the next section) and it is okay to be that way. Students who do not feel they fit in, or are depressed, use to escape those feelings.

Another major set of self-destructive behaviors is eating disorders. Anorexia, bulimia and over-/compulsive-eating are three ways to destroy your body and your health. This is not a newsflash. There is also physical harm, such as cutting, and psychological harm, such as self-induced depression.

These are just some of the ways people push the self-destruct button. If you are going through these, please seek help from a counselor at your school. You will probably need some help to get back on track (and that is what they are there to do). You should know that pretty much everyone has been self-destructive at some point in their lives. No one is proud of it. In fact, some will never speak of it because they are so ashamed. But know that you are so not alone.

Staying out of self-destruct mode can be tricky. To combat the enemies of self, think of these years as a giant shopping spree (sorry if this is too girly for some; bear with me here). You are going to try on many things (majors, friends, etc.). Some will fit, some will not. Sometimes you have to try on ten things before you find the right style and fit for you. You have a choice in this process:

1. Doubt yourself every time something does not work for you

OR

2. Have the great adventure of discovering who you are and what works for you.

Personality

We are all born with different characteristics. Sometimes it takes a while to discover who we are and where we are comfortable. We will explore different aspects of personality in this section, looking at some basic themes. [1][2]

Note that no one is really completely one-sided. Everyone has times when they are strong in one area and other times when they are stronger in another. Weaknesses should also not be used as crutches, "I can't help it, I'm ___ " Ideally, you should use this information to help yourself be more successful and give you a greater understanding of your strengths and your weaknesses.

One more thing: None of these sides are bad or better than the other. They are simply different ends of the spectrum. The headings for each of the areas are listed on either ends of a continuum. You will fall somewhere on the line (probably closer to one end than the other).

"If a man [or woman] has a talent and cannot use it, he [or she] has failed. If he [or she] has a talent and uses only half of it, he [or she] has partly failed. If he [or she] has a talent and learns somehow to use the whole of it, he [or she] has gloriously succeeded and has a satisfaction and a triumph few men [or women] ever know."
Thomas Wolfe (1900-1938), American Novelist

Extraverts_____Introverts

This aspect of your personality explains where you get your energy. Extraverts are those who are energized by being with other people. Extraverts might feel a bit more tired when they are by themselves, but look out when someone comes over for a visit. On the other hand, Introverts are those who get their energy from being by themselves. Although they may thoroughly enjoy being with other people, Introverts will tend to get worn out when around people for too long.

Although many Introverts may seem quiet and shy and Extraverts may seem outgoing, that will not always be the case. Some Extraverts are rather quiet; however they still get energized when around people. Likewise, some Introverts may be very outspoken; they will just need to recharge when they are around people for too long.

Dreamers_____Realists

This area refers to how you see the world. Some look around and see possibilities, others look around and see the world as it is. Dreamers are constantly thinking about how to grow or build something and are abstract thinkers, often our visionaries. They will always show us where we could be or could go next.

The Realists, on the other hand, tend to see what is practical. The Dreamer can hand them a vision and the Realist will know which parts will work and which will not. Realists believe in what they can see, hear, smell, touch, and taste. Both of these types can be creative. The Realists are more apt to create something new by combining experiences in a new way. The Dreamer may come up with something they, nor anyone else for that matter, has ever experienced.

Dreamer: "I think we can easily get 100 people to join our organization this year."

Realist: "We have seven right now."

Dreamer: "Yeah, but everyone is going to want to join this year."

Realist: "Well, I think if we did our marketing right and all seven of us pitched in, we could certainly increase our numbers."

Too far a Dreamer and you'll have nothing to show; too far a Realist and you'll have no place to go. It is very easy with these two to see how one may think the other is out of his or her mind. But the truth is, together they can accomplish so very much. If they really listen to one another, they will more than likely find a way to get nearly 100 people to join their organization this year. If they don't listen to each other, they will probably have four next year.

Logics_____Feelers

Here we are exploring how decisions are made. Logics base decisions on facts and tend to be more objective. Feelers base decisions on how they feel about something and tend to be more subjective.

Logics can seem, especially to a Feeler, cold, calculating and harsh. On the other hand, to the Logic, Feelers can appear over-emotional, illogical and too soft. In business, the Logics are the task-oriented folks. Their main goal is to get the job done and done well. The Feelers are the people-oriented ones. Their main goal is for everyone to get along and enjoy what they are doing.

I am sure that you can see the good and the bad in both. What good is a leader who gets the work completed, but at the end of the day is disliked by all? Or what good is a leader whom everyone loves, but gets nothing done?

The best thing a leader can do here is to find their opposite and listen to them. A word of warning, the vocabulary these types use tend to actually be different. A Logic, for example, may ask, "What do you think of this?" Leaving a Feeler to say, "I'm not sure what I think until I've considered those involved." A Feeler on the other hand might ask, "How do you feel about the solution?" To this a Logic is likely to think, "Uh... What do my feelings have to do with it? It's the right thing to do, so we do it."

Both are basically asking the same type of question; they are just coming at it from a different angle. If you get too caught up in the words, you may miss the point each is trying to make.

Organizers_____Experiencers

This aspect involves how you manage your life and time. There is a great big world out there. Do you want to put it in order and create an agenda for exploring it? Or do you want to hop in a car and go where the wind blows? Organizers are those who love agendas and color-codings. They prefer to know what is going to happen, before it happens.

On the other hand, Experiencers are those who want only to experience the world as it comes. They are more what might be called free spirits. They prefer not to have set schedules or anything too planned out. They will find it constraining. Again, we can see that having a compliment of both would be helpful.

"The meeting of two personalities is like the contact of two chemical substances;
If there is any reaction, both are transformed."
Carl Jung (1875-1961),
Swiss Psychologist/
Psychiatrist

Perception

We are all products of our:

Nature - what has always been our personality since we were born

Nurture - what our parents, grandparents, teachers, etc. taught us

Environment - where we are from, who our friends were and what experiences we have had

      Here's a bold statement: We only see what our experiences have taught us to see. Things outside of what we know are generally not seen by us immediately. Our nature and our nurture also play a role in our perception. They influence what we call a thing and whether we call it good or bad.

      So, is it good or bad that we don't see everything? I call it good. If you tried to take in everything and knew everything about everything, I'm pretty sure your brain would explode at some point. Well, perhaps not explode, but you would need no one but yourself in this world. You would know it all and see it all, and therefore need only yourself to assess any situation. But, as this is not the case, we do only see a part of the whole. In the next section, we will explore how we can see the rest of the picture.

> "We see things not as they are,
> but as we are"
> Anthony de Mello (1931-1987),
> Jesuit Priest from India

Diversity

When we hear the word diversity we tend to think about race, religion, gender differences, etc. Though all of those issues are important, they are only a fraction of what makes us diverse.

In the sections before this, we have been exploring self. You are, or are going to become, a leader. In doing so, others will know who you are. Before you let them know, it's always good to know yourself. I am sure that reading through the personality section, you found some of your strengths and some areas that were not your strengths. Notice, I didn't use the word "weakness." There is a difference between a weakness and something that is simply not your strength. In our society, we tend to think that if it is not one, it must be the other. I'm challenging you to think differently though. A weakness is something that you need to survive that you don't have. Something that is not your strength is simply an opportunity for someone else's strength to come through. Isn't it freeing to know you do not have to be good at everything?

> "We must learn to live together as brothers or perish as fools."
> Martin Luther King Jr.
> (1929-1968), American Civil Rights Activist & Leader

Living in a diverse world with so many different types of people, different perceptions, different ways of thinking, feeling and acting, as well as color, religion and lifestyle, makes this world the great place it is. Though any difference in opinion can cause some friction, ultimately differences are what make our world grow and become stronger. If we all agreed on everything and had the same personalities, we would be drones. We are not.

We are each unique individuals who have something to give to the world. You may be an Organizer, and the Experiencer is needed to show you how to handle the unpredictable parts of this world. You may be a Dreamer, and the Realist will help make those dreams come true through application. We are only a piece of the whole; we can only see the world from our own perceptions. By embracing others and their uniqueness, we, in effect, get to see the rest of the picture.

Leadership Styles

With all of the theories on leadership styles out there today, it can be confusing to try to figure out what style works. It is important to understand your natural tendency, as well as the ideal for being productive and having a happy team. We will be looking at two dimensions of leadership styles – how 'people focused' the leader is and how 'task focused' the leader is.

A "people focused" leader will show concern for the people he or she is leading. This leader is focused on ensuring that everyone is doing what suits their individual talents, that the morale is high and that everyone's needs are being met.

"The man who makes no mistakes does not usually make anything."
Edward Phelps (1822-1900), Lawyer & Diplomat from Vermont

A "task focused" leader, on the other hand, will show concern for the task he or she is meant to complete. It is about the job at hand. This leader is focused on ensuring that the task is done right and completed on time. Most leaders are some combination of both of these types. [3]

Comparing the two styles:

❋ A person who is only "people focused" and not "task focused" may be well liked, but probably won't get much done.

❋ A person who is only "task focused" and not "people focused" will probably get the job done, but may not be so well liked.

❋ A person who is neither "people-" nor "task focused" probably won't get much done nor will be liked much.

❋ *The best version, of course, is a person who shows concern for people and yet stays focused on the task. It's all about the balance.*

But, balancing the two can be tricky at times. Here are some things to keep in mind:

- Without people to help, you could not accomplish as much. They will not only help get projects done faster, but will also help make them better.

- People want to feel appreciated for their efforts. If something is ultimately done incorrectly, it may be difficult to acknowledge the work that they did on it. However, if you want them to continue to work for you, you must be sure they know you appreciate their efforts.

- Be sure that your expectations are clearly defined. You can't blame your team for not understanding what you wanted if you don't tell them what you wanted. Expectations allow you to empower the people in your group. You say, "Here are the guidelines and goals, now–enjoy." They are allowed the freedom to make decisions (as long as they stay within the guidelines).

- Let people do the job you have asked them to do. If people feel as if someone is standing over them, they will not give you their best.

- Stay on task. Taking little breaks here and there is fine, however you want to be sure that you are moving towards the final product.

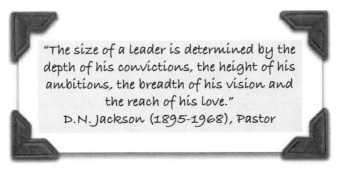

"The size of a leader is determined by the depth of his convictions, the height of his ambitions, the breadth of his vision and the reach of his love."
D.N. Jackson (1895-1968), Pastor

Characteristics of a Leader

There is no clear–cut, agreed–upon definition of a leader or what a leader should be. However, there are some aspects of leadership that seem to run deep in all good leaders. Your character is a critical factor in whether people choose to follow you and for how long they will follow you. In this chapter, we explore many qualities or characteristics that all great leaders seem to have in common.

> "Whatever we learn to do, we learn by actually doing it: Men come to be builders, for instance, by building, and harp players by playing the harp. In the same way, by doing just acts, we come to be just; by doing self-controlled acts, we come to be self-controlled; and by doing brave acts, we come to be brave."
> Aristotle (384 BC– 322 BC),
> Philosopher & Teacher

Perspective

At times one event can seem like it is the be all and end all event. One night can seem like the only night that matters. But by the next day or so, that event can seem like old news. Such intense moments will happen constantly in life. Trying not to react immediately to situations when emotions have been stirred can save a lot of heartache. If you wait and think about the situation for a bit, your reaction might be very different. If you look at a situation from another's point of view or as part of a larger picture, you can reel in much of the anger and frustration.

There is a painting technique, called pointillism, which uses small dots to create the picture itself. A bunch of dots in one area, for example, may turn out to be a tree or an eye. As the painter is painting, he or she is only working on one dot at a time. It is only after the artist has made a series of dots, that he or she can stand back and see the final product. This is very similar to our lives. Everything we do, every day, represents one dot. It is easy for us, as the artists of our lives, to get so focused on the one dot that we forget about the totality of the painting we are creating. At those times, it is best for us to step back and regain our vision of the big picture and realize – that dot, is just one dot amongst many.

Integrity

Integrity is a strong commitment to a moral or ethical code. People want to follow those they can trust. Don't you? Those who follow you want to know they can count on their leader, their leader is looking out for their best interest, and their leader is honest and genuine. Nobody is perfect and nobody expects a leader to be perfect. People do, however, expect a leader to do the best he or she can, to do what needs to be done and admit mistakes. Trust is one of the most fragile and critical bonds we can have with others. If violated, trust is very hard to regain. As a leader, one should do his or her best to maintain a high level of integrity. Integrity leads to respect, which leads to trust. It's all about doing the right thing.

Courage

Courage is NOT being fearless. Where there is no fear, there is no need of courage. Courage is doing what it takes despite the fear or opposition. Courage also means you won't always know the outcome. Standing up for what you believe in, en*courag*ing others to do the same, making tough decisions... all take courage. Every great leader since the beginning of time has shown courage. It takes courage to start something new; it takes courage to continue the thing; it takes courage to stay the leader when, at times, it may be lonely up there.

Discipline

Discipline is doing what you are supposed to do, regardless of whether you feel like it or not. It is an interesting quality. You see, we don't always feel like doing what we know we should do. But, discipline means we do it anyway because it needs to be done. This is where our "inner parent" comes in. Discipline is one major sign of maturity! Here's the cool thing about it... You only have to really force yourself to stay this way for a relatively short time. After a while, being disciplined becomes like second nature– it just seems normal and we no longer even think about it.

Motivation

Motivation is what separates the ordinary from the extraordinary! Phase one of motivation requires that the leader be motivated. Everyone has something to give to the world, something great to leave for future generations. But many will never join in, either as a leader or a group member, and thus fail to make a difference. They simply are not motivated. It amazes me to think that if everyone were motivated to make the world better, what a world we might be living in. Our world needs motivated individuals to make a difference.

Once self-motivated, phase two is motivating others. Here are a few hints:

1. When motivating others, using emotional words or appealing to their emotions will work fast– but only for a limited time.

2. When motivating others, appealing to their logic takes a while– but will have lasting effects.

3. When motivating others, using someone they know and trust as their motivator, you can expect it to work for some and last as long as they still trust the motivator.

4. The best motivation techniques use all of the above. If you are the motivator, make sure that people *trust you* (see Integrity!), have them *feel the cause* and make sure they *know exactly why* they should do this (both emotionally and logically).

5. The only way to *truly keep people motivated* is for them to adopt the cause and own it.

Fortitude

Fortitude is stick-to-it-iveness. No matter how hard you work in life, or how pure your motives, there will be times when life will hand you a lemon! That's just the nature of living. You will probably have times when what you are doing is not the most popular thing to do or times when everything seems to be going wrong. Then there will be times when you just don't feel like doing much. Continuing to "stick-to-it" is not an easy task, but it will make the end result all the more rewarding.

Balance

Without balance in our lives, it's like leaving a light bulb on 24/7; we burn out pretty quickly. Balance often takes some discipline at first. We should be sure to have relatively equal amounts of work, play, and rest. Making sure you're getting the right foods, enough exercise, some intellectual stimulation, personal and social time, ensures a more whole person. If we sink all of our energy into one area, we don't go very far. Always take time for yourself. Learn something every day. Don't overwork or under-work yourself. If you can do these things, you will maintain the wellness necessary to be a great leader!

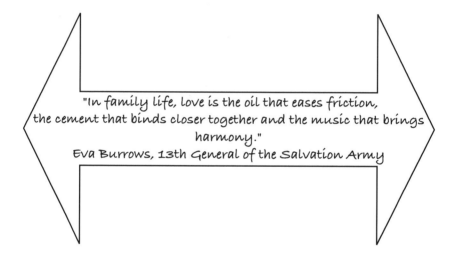

"In family life, love is the oil that eases friction, the cement that binds closer together and the music that brings harmony."
Eva Burrows, 13th General of the Salvation Army

Family

Every great leader seems to have a sense of family. They work to make sure that the team feels like a family. They make sure that the team still has time to be with their own families.

A family supports you through thick and thin. For your team to stay strong, it is important that they feel they can always depend on the team. Members will give more of themselves because they are supported.

Spirituality/Love/Growth

Regardless of whether or not you are religious, there is an underlying aspect of spirituality or love that amazing leaders have. Leaders care deeply for those who follow them. Leaders want their team to grow and reach their potential. Reaching one's potential is a life-time journey. Sometimes the road is fun and sometimes it is very difficult.

All living things (including humans) need to grow. A seed must become a tree and the tree must grow to its full potential. Have you ever seen a tree that has twisted so it could reach the light? That tree has a hunger to reach its potential. A true leader works to help each team member realize his or her individual potential. When someone feels fulfilled, they do not hunger for more. He or she is constantly getting that need met and therefore finds no reason to look elsewhere for that growth.

Delegation

As a leader, you are responsible for many things. One area, often overlooked, is to take care of you and not overdo it. Leaders tend to be those who want to get things done. Followers do not necessarily feel the same way. Therefore, leaders may find themselves doing too much. It is easier just to do it yourself. However, this is not the best long-term option. Doing everything by yourself can lead to:

✺ Burn-out and exhaustion.

✺ Members not feeling like they have a vital role and assuming that they are not needed.

✺ Members not growing and learning.

Every strong leader, at some point, learns to delegate. Learning to depend on and trust your team is a key to getting the best jobs done right and on time. Some new leaders may feel that by allowing others to do so many tasks, there will be nothing for the leader themselves to do. Delegating does NOT mean just telling someone that he or she is responsible for a giant task, then walking away. True delegation empowers others, provides a framework and the time for you to be a servant leader.

A great delegator and servant leader will:

❈ Provide support: This might be training, supplies, or anything needed to get the job done.

❈ Clarifying objectives: Being sure that everyone is on the same page.

❈ Maintaining relationships: NOT forgetting to say "thank you," or "great job," or "How are you?"

❈ Follow-up: Checking in with people along the way.

Being Proactive

We all have a choice whether to set ourselves up to succeed or to fail.   Being proactive is the art of setting up your own success. And it's not as hard as it may sound. You know what you want in the long-run. All you have to do is take the necessary steps to get there. This also means taking as few counter-productive steps as possible along the way.

Doing what you know is right may not always be popular with others, but it will make sure that you stay on your path to success. If you want to be a doctor, being proactive means getting the right grades, etc., to eventually get into medical school. To be proactive, one must look ahead. It also means figuring out what could go wrong and accounting for it. Everything we do has a way of coming back around to us. What do you want to come back to you?

"Believe while others are doubting. Plan while others are playing. Study while others are sleeping. Decide while others are delaying. Prepare while others are daydreaming. Begin while others are procrastinating. Work while others are wishing. Save while others are wasting. Listen while others are talking. Smile while others are frowning. Commend while others are criticizing. Persist while others are quitting."
William Arthur Ward (1921-1994), Author

Attitude

The attitude of the leader = the atmosphere/climate of the group. If the leader has a positive, can-do attitude, so will the team. If the leader complains, the group will reciprocate. Showing that the project is important to you, by your actions, will help the team feel that the project is important. Plus, the more energy and enthusiasm with which you do your tasks, the more gusto your team will have in doing their own portions of the project.

Attitude really does trickle down. So if you are at the top (or even close to it), what you say and how you say it can not only affect your current project, but how others feel about the entire organization.

> "The greatest discovery in our generation is that human beings, by changing the inner attitudes of their minds, can change the outer aspects of their lives."
> William James (1842-1910)
> US Philosopher & Psychologist

Role Models and Mentors

Every great leader has at least one great role model and/or mentor. No one is born knowing everything there is to know about leading. We watch others, we imitate others, we learn from others. Role models do just that– they model a role for us. Whether we personally know our role model or follow him or her on Twitter/ in the news/ on screen, we should all be intentional about selecting who our role models are. In selecting a role model, then, it would make sense that we first understand what role we would like modeled. If your goal is to be a leader, then that is the role. Now select someone that models that well.

A mentor, on the other hand, is someone who has more knowledge and wisdom in an area that you are striving to grow in. You can talk to that person, ask questions and learn from a personal relationship. This can be very helpful, especially at times when you may not know exactly what to do or are feeling discouraged.

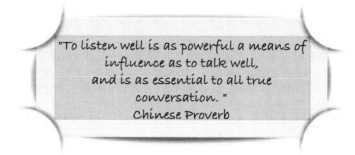

"To listen well is as powerful a means of influence as to talk well, and is as essential to all true conversation."
Chinese Proverb

Influence

They say that imitation is the greatest form of flattery. Meaning that if people look up to you, they will emulate (or copy) what you do in many different areas of your life. For example, if the "cool" kid at school talks back to his or her teachers, others will do the same. If that same kid treats a teacher with respect, others will do likewise.

Part of being a leader is understanding your power to influence. Everything you do is watched and can be imitated, from a particular hairstyle to behavior. If, as a leader of a particular group, you do something you know is not safe, you could, in effect, lead others to harm. If, however, you do your best to be your best, you can actually help others to increase their self-esteem and self-worth. You really do have the power. The question is… what do you plan to do with it?

Here are a few ways we influence others.

❋ Artifacts: What you wear, how you fix your hair, jewelry, etc.

❋ Behaviors: What you do. This includes what you choose to do in your free time, how you act in school, etc.

❋ Treatment of others: Whether or not you gossip about so and so. Also, how you treat the "cool" kids versus the "nerdy" kids. If you make fun of others as a leader, you show your followers that it is okay.

❋ Causes: There are issues that are important to all of us. But there is generally one or two that stick out as our own personal issues we wish to tackle.

Character Qualities

So many qualities can describe a leader. All of the qualities discussed in this chapter (and those listed at the end) are good for a leader to have. Is there a leader out there who has "it all?" Of course not... we're only human. Some of the qualities will come naturally to you, a part of your personality. Others will seem to be nearly impossible. Still others, you may feel, are within your reach, with a little practice.

For those areas you are naturally talented in, use those qualities to their utmost. Find a role or position in an organization that allows the "you of today" to shine. For other areas, find ways to practice them. Who we become in life is a product of our habitual choices and behaviors. If one consistently makes the choice, for example, to not worry about "being late today," eventually, it will never occur to that person to be respectful of other people's time.

On the other hand, if one decides that punctuality is important and one starts making an effort to plan and be on time, eventually, punctuality will become a normal part of his or her life. It does not mean that you will never mess up or never be late or never wish you could start your day over again. But every mess up is a chance to really evaluate why this did not go as you wished it had. Resolve that the next time you are in a similar situation, you will make the choice that leads you to success.

If you've ever taken a lesson on... well, just about anything, it is the same principle that applies here. You might be naturally gifted in music... but more than likely, you need to practice often to be your best.

"Watch your thoughts; they become your words. Watch your words; they become your actions. Watch your actions; they become your habits. Watch your habits; they become your character. Watch your character for it will become your destiny."
Unknown

Here is a list of qualities for you, a leader, to explore. My suggestion is to look through the list (take your time), and think about how each one of these qualities would help you in your life and in leadership. If you don't know what one of them means, look it up. It is worth it!

Acceptance	**Accountability**	**Action-Oriented**
Alertness	**Assertiveness**	**Attentiveness**
Availability	**Balance**	**Boldness**
Candor	**Cautiousness**	**Citizenship**
Commitment	**Compassion**	**Confidence**
Consistency	**Contentment**	**Courage**
Courtesy	**Creativity**	**Cultured**
Decisiveness	**Deference**	**Dependability**
Determination	**Diligence**	**Discernment**
Discipline	**Discretion**	**Endurance**
Enthusiasm	**Fairness**	**Faith**
Firmness	**Flexibility**	**Forgiveness**
Fortitude	**Friendliness**	**Generosity**
Goal-Oriented	**Graciousness**	**Gratefulness**
Honesty	**Hope**	**Hospitality**

Humility	Humor	Initiative
Integrity	Joyfulness	Justice
Kindness	Knowledge	Love
Loyalty	Manners	Motivation
Openness	Optimism	Organization
Originality	Passion	Patience
Peacefulness	Perseverance	Persuasiveness
Poise	Healthy Pride	Proactive
Prudence	Punctuality	Reliability
Resourcefulness	Responsibility	Self-Control
Self-Discipline	Self-Respect	Sensitivity
Servanthood	Sincerity	Sportsmanship
Supportive	Teachability	Thoroughness
Thoughtfulness	Thriftiness	Tolerance
Trustworthiness	Truthfulness	Vision
Vulnerability	Wisdom	Wonderment

Effective Communication Skills

Listening

Listening and hearing are NOT the same thing. Hearing is a biological process we can't help but do. Listening on the other hand, involves our brain and thinking. One of the best-kept secrets of being a good leader is the ability to listen (and not just hear) what is going on in- and outside of your team. Below is a list of effective listening techniques you can begin to use today. [4]

✺ *Find a way to be interested*. There will be plenty of times when someone is talking about a topic that doesn't interest you in the least… at first glance. But there will rarely, if ever, be a time when someone is talking about a topic that won't benefit you in some way. One of the keys to being a good listener is to find that benefit!

✺ *Get over the speaker's appearance or delivery*. Not everyone will be a super-model, grade "A" speaker. In fact, most of us aren't. But that doesn't mean we don't have something important or interesting to say. A good listener is one who looks beyond those things and focuses on what is being said.

✺ *Ignore distractions*. OK. So the universe is a busy place with a lot going on. And yes, it is easy to get distracted by actual noises or just stuff we're thinking about (daydreaming). Setting all of that aside and paying attention to what the other person is saying is a sure way to let them know they are important to you and for you to truly understand what they are saying.

✺ *Listen for the big picture*. When we listen for just the facts, we tend to focus on one or two items instead of the whole message. Sometimes what a person is really saying has to do more with how they are feeling, and if we just pay attention to a few things they've said, we could miss that.

✹ *Stop faking attention*. We all pretend to listen sometimes and that can get us into trouble. The reason we do this is generally because we think a lot faster than the other person can talk (about four times faster)! The key here is to use that extra time to really understand what is being said and somehow relate it to your own life. Connecting it to something that you've already experienced will help you recall it later as well.

✹ *Hold back your judgment*. Everyone has "trigger" words or topics, ones that stir up emotions. When we fall victim to those words and let them get us worked up, we are no longer listening. If we hold off on the emotions until the whole message is finished, many times we realize that the other person didn't mean any harm or maybe meant something entirely different than we thought.

✹ *Embrace what is over your head*. No matter how old or educated we are, we WILL come into contact with difficult topics (quantum physics, Shakespeare, etc.). Most people tend to avoid what is difficult for them, while motivated people do their best to understand it. Not everyone will be a scientist or a literary scholar, but we can exercise our minds and continue to grow always. And, if you think about it, embracing what is over our heads is how we've been learning new things all of our lives. Who knows, you may learn something really cool or grasp a concept that has always baffled you!

"Listen a hundred times; ponder a thousand times; speak once."
Turkish Proverb

Communicating Without Words

People believe what we say, right? Not necessarily. In fact, only about 7% of what people believe actually comes from the words we say. The other 93% is based on something called nonverbal communication. Successful leaders are those who use nonverbal communication effectively and who can read other people. Here are a few ways, other than with words, we communicate with others. [5]

Body Movements and Gestures

These tell us how excited, nervous, and emotional someone is, as well as help us get our entire message across. They include things like talking with our hands, how much we move around, our posture, etc.

Facial Expressions and Eye Behavior

Facial expressions tell about people's emotions, interpretations, and judgments. Eye contact usually gives us a clue of the other person's honesty and how interested they are in what we are saying.

Voice

Our tone pretty much tells the other person how to take what we are saying. It tells them how we are feeling and how they should feel about our message.

Clothing and Personal Artifacts

This includes clothing, jewelry, make-up, hairstyles, shoes, nails, etc. Everything you choose to put on says something about you. Whether good or bad, you can guess something about someone's personality or attitude by what they are wearing.

Time and Space

The way we use our time and whether or not we are on time says a great deal about our priorities. We tend to be on time and make time for things that are important to us. If you are not making time for something in your life, it may be wise to evaluate its true importance to you.

How close we stand to others and how much we touch are also important factors. In general, the closer we are physically, the closer we are emotionally. E.T. Hall, a theorist, came up with a scale to judge space– these are only general measurements; yours may vary. From 0"-18" is our intimate space (best friends, family, etc.), 18"- 4' is our interpersonal space (acquaintances, classmates, etc.), 4'-12' is our social space (small groups, etc.), and 12'+ is public space (we don't care who is there). We tend to get uncomfortable when the people invade the wrong space. [6]

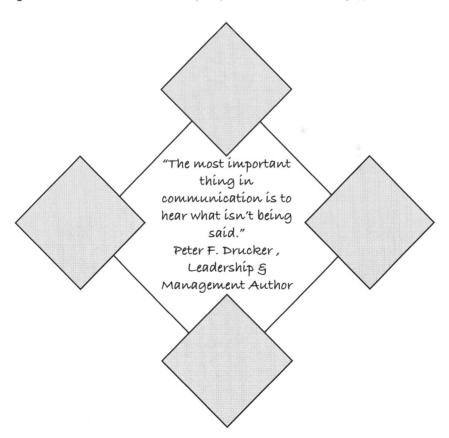

"The most important thing in communication is to hear what isn't being said."
Peter F. Drucker, Leadership & Management Author

Intercultural Communication

> "The hardest part about growing up is letting go of what you have been accustomed to and moving on with something that you haven't experienced yet."
> Unknown

Communication is culturally unique, including our spoken language, our written language, even how we interpret nonverbal cues. Most of us are aware that face to face communication with people from another culture will probably be different than your own. The only thing that all cultures have in common is emotion and the show of emotion. A smile is the same in any language.

Having said that, we must now keep in mind that with the advent of the internet and world-wide media, our newest generations are starting to communicate in more similar patterns across the cultures. As students from different countries chat online or chat while gaming, we are starting to see less culturally unique communication and more generationally unique communication. This will be explained in greater detail in the "Unique 2U" section.

This phenomenon may also provide a bit of a shock when meeting someone from a particular culture in person for the first time, where communication may have been mostly electronic in the past. Different expectations with regard to time usage, personal space, eye behavior, etc. are certainly not experienced in the same way in the virtual world. These are tied strongly to a person's culture of origin. If there is something that you don't understand with regard to someone's culture, ask. Most people are very happy to share their beliefs and background with others who are truly interested.

> "We all should know that diversity makes for a rich tapestry, and we must understand that all the threads of the tapestry are equal in value no matter what their color."
> Maya Angelou, American Author & Poet

Speeches

> "My father gave me these hints on speech-making:
> Be sincere... be brief... be seated."
> James Roosevelt (1907-1991), US Rep, military officer & son of FDR

Giving a speech can be one of the most frightening experiences! If you go to school or are involved with anything, ever... you will probably have to give a speech at some point. Rather than making yourself sick about it, here are some things you can do to help ease the stress of speech-giving.

Speech Tips

※ A good night's *sleep* and a good *breakfast* help you feel and speak with more energy and to be prepared both mentally and physically.

※ *Dress* appropriately and professionally. Plus, the better you look, the better you feel, the better you'll speak.

※ Make a good complete *outline* of your speech (see "Speech Structure Outline"). When you give your speech, note cards can be too small and cumbersome to use, unless you are very accustomed to them. Try using normal size or legal size paper for your notes, and write big or with a larger font size (Like 20pt).

※ Use main points and thoughts in your outline, *avoiding complete sentences* (unless every word must be exact). This will help you sound more conversational and resist the urge to read your speech (which can negatively affect your eye contact and delivery).

※ *Do not chew gum* and *take off your hat* when you speak. Your image and mannerisms are important. Impressions of you are formed the second you go on stage.

※ *Practice, Practice, Practice.* Design and plan your speeches ahead of time (before the night before). You'll have more time to practice and time your speech.

Delivery Tips

※ Know your introduction and key points well, allowing you to give your audience lots of eye contact. Try to avoid reading long segments of your speech.

※ Avoid cursing and slang.

※ Relax!!! If you prepare, are organized, and practice, you can be confident that you will do well.

※ Transition your audience from one point to the next.

※ Make eye contact with as many of the audience members as possible.

※ Use your natural hand gestures, facial expressions…let your personality show. Don't be afraid to smile, when appropriate, and express yourself.

※ Speak clearly and loudly enough for everyone in the room to hear you. Be sure to pronounce all words correctly, particularly names of others.

※ Visualize your speech as being successful before you give it. Believe in yourself and others will believe in you too!

"Make sure you have finished speaking before your audience has finished listening."
Dorothy Sarnoff (1914-2008), Opera singer, Broadway star & self-help guru

Speech Structure Outline

I. Introduction

A.   Attention-getter (quotes, rhetorical questions, jokes, etc.).

B.   Establish a connection with the audience.

C.   Establish the importance/relevance of your speech to your audience.

D. Preview the content of your speech.

II. Body of the Speech

A. 2-4 main points/ideas in a typical speech, but this will vary

B. Use an organized sequence for your ideas (chronological, topical, spacial, etc.). Help the listener follow your speech by organizing your ideas logically.

C. Include plenty of supports for the information you present (explanation/definitions, testimony, statistics, illustrations, etc.).

III. Conclusion

A. Summary/review.

B. Bring speech back around to the audience.

C. Call the audience to action (where to go from here).

D. Note of finality (quote, final thought, etc.)

Other Aspects to Consider

Audience Analysis   To whom are you speaking?

✸ Know your audience (age, interests, sex, attitude)

✸ Plan for them- *the audience is the most important, not the speaker...their* understanding is *your* goal and focus.

Visual Aids   (Overheads, PowerPoint, handouts, charts, etc.)

✸ They must be visual and they must aid you in some way. Sounds simple, but includes: making sure your font is large enough and neat enough for the people in back to read, that your aid is not too cluttered, that it is relevant to your topic and that it is something that is useful for the audience to see (unless your speech is on the making of a soccer ball, where you need to point out the stitching, etc., a soccer ball makes a poor aid, since we all know what it looks like– Your aid should aid in the understanding of something). Numbers and statistics are generally good visual aids.

✸ They can really help your presentation look professional.

✸ Always test and proofread them before you do the real thing.

✸ Be intentional about when you present your aid. If you are doing handouts, be aware that people will look at them, not you, when you pass them out. So be sure you don't pass them out until you need to.

Delivery Coming across the right way

❋ Gestures/Eye Contact

❋ Force yourself to use them. Use a friendly, conversational style.

❋ Open gestures (wrists out) are generally best.

❋ Movement/Posture
❋ Don't be afraid to move around a little; you don't want to look planted. The podium is an option, just don't clench it.

❋ Take a few steps for big ideas, or emphasis.

❋ Voice/Diction

❋ The more articulate you are, the more intelligent and credible you will sound. Take your time when speaking and enunciate.

❋ Project your voice so that all can hear you clearly.

❋ Try to limit the number of pauses and fillers (ums) between ideas (use pauses for dramatic effects). Practice helps here.

"There are always three speeches, for every one you actually gave. The one you practiced, the one you gave, and the one you wish you gave."
Dale Carnegie,
Author, Public Speaking Trainer

Comm Unique 2U

As you well know, communication is changing before our eyes. We are in a relatively new age where instant access to information is commonplace and constant communication is expected. With this have come some amazing tools that can be both wonderfully helpful or can hurt you in one way or another… depending on how you utilize them. Here are a few things to consider about today's technologies.

Online Profiles

Social networking sites offer us the chance to create an autobiography for all to see. They offer a way to connect to others who have similar interests, belong to the same organizations or live in the same area. Privacy settings allow us to keep our information amongst "friends;" however, once a "friend," someone can find out– who our friends are, what groups we belong to, what our favorite movies, music, and quotes are, our pictures– anything that we and/or others post. Today, employers, college recruiters, teachers, parents, and more are looking at our pages. Sometimes, this determines whether or not we get an interview… Fair? Perhaps not, but it is reality. You have an opportunity to use your profile pages as tools to help market yourself, your interests, your skills, your wit, and more. Think of it as your really cool business card.

"Skill in the art of communication is crucial to a leader's success. He can accomplish nothing unless he can communicate effectively."
Norman Allen (1947-2009)
"Stormin' Norman",
NBA player & television sportscaster

Blogs, Et Cetera

Generations before will never quite understand. There was a book (you may have heard of it), George Orwell's *1984*, that brought forth the idea of someone watching you, always knowing what you are doing, thinking, saying… To anyone who read that book, prior to 1984, the daylights were scared out of them that someone would invade their privacy. You have grown up with the internet, with openly sharing your thoughts, dreams, pictures, etc. This is not necessarily a bad thing; however, those older generations may have a point too. You should always be aware, and post as if, your friends and family and those with good intentions are not necessarily the only ones reading your profiles and blogs. So, please be careful and choose what you share wisely.

Txting, IMing, Msging, etc.

Instant communication has created a new shorthand (an old way of taking quick notes) and reduced, if not obliterated, punctuation and structure. I'm not calling it bad. It is what it is and it's a lot easier to type on my phone using it. Just another heads up, though… those from generations prior to yours are not necessarily ready for the change (nor do they need to be– it's who *they* are and it's okay). When composing emails (which is still the generally accepted official channel for business and academic communication), go back and use the grammar and punctuation you learned all those years in school. Also, because former generations grew up without instant communication, they may not get back to you within the hour. Don't worry if you haven't had a response the same day (unless it is a real emergency). You will get a much better response from professors and others if you keep these things in mind. But, by all means, use ur txt w/ ur bff & those who understand it.

COLLEGE 101

College is very different from high school. Aside from the obvious, (it's usually larger and costs more money), administration is also structured differently and all of sudden you're taking "hours." This can be confusing. Schools will vary on what they call something (a title of a job or a specific office), but there are some things relatively common to all.

From applying for financial aid to how colleges are structured to explaining what those "hours" mean, this chapter will give you a brief overview of college. The topics in this chapter are here because these are the questions students going into college had, when I asked them what they wanted to know.

> "Education makes a people easy to lead,
> but difficult to drive;
> easy to govern,
> but impossible to enslave."
> Baron Henry Peter Brougham
> (1778-1868), British political leader

Scholarships and Financial Aid

As you already know college can become expensive! Scholarships of any amount of money can help you and your family from having to find ways to pay for college, for example, student loans. Opportunities for scholarships are nearly endless; however, these opportunities are not always easily earned or easily found. There are a few processes that students, like yourself, need to be familiar with before you begin searching for scholarship opportunities.

Personal Need Statement

Develop your personal need statement for scholarships. Your personal need statement may include any or all of the factors that follow. Read through the following questions, applying them to your life and decide which to include in your personal need statement.

❋ How many siblings do you have and how many of them will be in college at the same time?

❋ Will you be the first student in your family to attend college?

❋ Will you be attending a two-year or four-year university?

❋ Will you be attending college in state?

❋ Why are you applying for scholarships?

❋ Do you have achievements, awards, and involvements in your high school and community?

> "Education's purpose is to replace an empty mind with an open one."
> Malcolm S. Forbes (1919-1990), American business leader

❋ What are your short term and long term college and career goals?

An example of a personal need statement

"As the oldest of three siblings, I am the first child in my family to attend a four year in-state university. I am looking forward to continuing my active involvement during my college career. By receiving scholarships, I will be able to assist my parents with the cost of college and achieve my goal of being debt free when I graduate from college. "

Scholarship Calendar

As with any planning, it is helpful to have a calendar to plan out what needs to be done and when. Scholarship applications will typically become available during the late summer and early in the fall semester, with deadlines around February or March. The early deadlines allow scholarship review committees to review the scholarships and choose a recipient during the spring to apply toward your freshman year of college. These deadlines are generalizations for most scholarships.

When you get any scholarship application, review the application requirements and deadlines. First, write on your calendar the deadline of the application. Second, if there are any letters of recommendation that are needed, write down the dates that you will ask for the letters of recommendation and the dates that you will pick up the letters of recommendation. This may not seem to be to important right now. However, you may have two or three scholarship applications that are due around the same time and need to plan carefully so that you are not confused or stressed.

> "If you think education is expensive, try ignorance."
> Derek Bok,
> Former president of Harvard University

FAFSA

Free Application for Federal Student Aid is a form to become familiar with during your scholarship searching. FAFSA is available on the internet at www.fafsa.ed.gov. The form will ask financial information about you and your family's income. The purpose of FAFSA is to see if you meet the qualifications for any financial aid assistance such as school assistance, student aid, and work study. Scholarship forms may require that you have simply completed the FAFSA form online before applying for their scholarship. FAFSA forms can be completed in early spring after receiving the tax information from the previous year. Additionally, the FAFSA deadline is in the early summer for the next school year. DO NOT delay completing the FAFSA form to avoid any future headaches! Through FAFSA, you may find you qualify for government grants. This is also where you will find information about student loans and work-study.

Where to Look for Scholarships

❀ *Internet*. The internet is a great place to start searching for scholarships. Several internet search engines offer students the opportunity to search for scholarships on their database. You DO NOT need to pay for any scholarship search! A majority of scholarship search engines or websites will ask that you complete a user profile including questions on your interests, your major in college, and your involvement at school or community. They will then compare your profile with the scholarships that are listed with their search engine. The comparison will compile a list of scholarships which you qualify for based on your scholarship profile. Scholarships that are listed on the internet are often nationwide scholarships and award various amounts of money. Here are two good search engines, to get you started: www.fastweb.com, www.college-scholarships.com.

❀ *University*. Many universities have a scholarship application for incoming freshman. This application is often simple to complete, asking for personal contact information, your decided major, and possibly essay questions. Contact the scholarship office at the university or universities that you are considering attending early in the fall semester to see about scholarship opportunities.

❀ *Community*. Often many groups in your local community will award scholarships to graduating high school seniors based on their academic achievement and community involvement. Examples of these community groups include: American Legion and American Legion Auxiliary, Boy Scouts and Girl Scouts, church organizations, Masonic Lodge, and Rotary Clubs.

※ *High School.* Your high school will likely have an office for college and careers, a counseling center, or student sponsor office where you can find scholarship applications as well.

※ *Family.* Surprisingly, your own family members are a great place to start searching for scholarships. Check with your parents or guardians to see if their employers offer scholarships to children of the employee. Also, check with your employer too about scholarship opportunities. It never hurts to ask!

> "Don't ever dare to take your college as a matter of course- because, like democracy and freedom, many people you'll never know have broken their hearts to get it for you." Alice Miller (1923-2010), Psychologist & author

Scholarship Application Etiquette

To scholarship review committees, everything they know about you is on a piece of paper. Often times this may be the only time that you are considered with these committees, if there is not an interview in the selection process. Keep in mind that you are being compared to other applicants. You want to look your very best on paper! Listed below are some areas of the application process to consider.

※ *Application.* The instructions on many applications ask that you print or type your application. To avoid any confusion in reading your handwriting, even if it is excellent, type your application. If the application is available online, type the application on your computer. If not, find a typewriter; there is usually one at your local library. Keep in mind that typing on a typewriter is different than a computer. The typewriter may not have spell check or the ability to erase an entire sentence. In this case it is helpful to make a copy of your original application and complete the copy of the application as a guide to completing the original copy on the typewriter. More than anything else, typing your scholarship application will show the scholarship selection committee that typing it was worth the investment of your time. Again, being compared to other scholarship applications, you want to have your application stand out because of completeness, following the instructions, professionalism, proper use of grammar, and overall presentation. If you have invested time and thought into your application this will work to your advantage! *Keep copies of all applications that you complete with all information that you turn in with the scholarship.*

✳ **Essays**. Save copies of these essays on your computer or on a flash drive. Once you have written a few essays, chances are that you are able to adapt what you have already written to fit multiple scholarship answers. You will be working smarter, not harder!

✳ **Letters of Recommendation**. These letters are usually written by people who know you fairly well (e.g. counselors, teachers, coaches, church leaders, and employers) and are able to write a personal letter to recommend you for the scholarship. Provide each of these individuals with a brief resume, what you would like the letter to emphasize, and a summary of the specific scholarship for which you are applying. Keep in mind that you may have several letters of recommendation for different scholarship applications due at one time. With that said, review your scholarship calendar and the due dates. Allow two weeks for the person you are asking to write your letter of recommendation. Set due dates for all letters of recommendation earlier than the scholarship deadline. This will ensure that you have all the letters on time. Because you may need many letters, it is helpful to choose several individuals who know you well to write the letters. Also, if you feel comfortable enough, you may ask some of these individuals writing the letter to allow you to reuse their letter for other scholarships.

Thank You Notes

It is important that you take the time to recognize the people who have helped you in preparation with your scholarships. A small thank you card or online message is appropriate to thank these individuals. Thank you cards are appropriate for recognizing anyone else who helped you in the scholarship searching process such as high school or college counselors, administrators, parents, teachers, etc. You should send thank you notes within two weeks from the time that you received the help or letter of recommendation from the person.

The Scoop on Taking Loans

After applying for scholarships, federal grants and figuring out what help you will receive from family, you may still be faced with an important financial decision: To take out a student loan or not? Here are some basic facts for you to consider when making your choice:

✻ Student loans can add up over the course of four years. You should consider whether you need all of what is offered or part of it.

✻ Student loans must be paid back after you graduate. You will get a small grace period to get on your feet, then you must pay back the loan or risk seriously injuring your credit score.

✻ Student loan interest is by far one of the lowest interest rates you will ever have. It is MUCH cheaper than say, charging on a credit card.

✻ In 2010, the unemployment rate for a high school grad was 10.3%. For a college grad (bachelor's degree) it dropped to 5.4% and for a professional degree (a degree for a particular profession, Master's level or above- M.D., J.D., counselor, nurse practitioner, etc.) it dropped to 2.4%! Therefore, when you finish school, you are more likely to be able to get a job. [7]

✳ In 2010, the average worker with a bachelor's degree earned nearly double what a person with a high school diploma earned. In other words, that job you get when you graduate from college should pay you enough to make your student loan payments. [7]

✳ If taking a loan for college means you can focus on your degree and not have to work fulltime, it is worth considering how much you are losing every year you do not graduate. For example: If you take a loan that allows you to graduate in four years, hopefully, by year five you are working in your chosen field, making enough to start paying back your loans... and maybe even saving for a down payment on your first house. If you have to work full time (and sometimes that is the case), it is likely to take several more years of school before graduation. That is several more years of not doing what it is you wish to do and not having the money to do more than make ends meet.

✳ It is not always an easy decision, but it is worth looking at all sides before you make your choice and decide what is right for you. The financial aid department on your campus may be able to help you weigh some of your options.

"Education is the key to unlock the golden door of freedom."
George Washington Carver (1864-1943), American scientist & inventor

Choosing and/or Changing Your Major

By far some of the most stressful topics for students revolve around their majors. What should I do? What if I don't like it? What if I change my mind? What if I go through all of this and end up not liking the field? What will my parents think of this career choice?

First, if you feel this way, you are not even close to being alone. It is rare for a student to enter college knowing just what he or she wants to do AND graduating with a degree to do exactly that. Second, this is part of what college is all about. You are supposed to explore many different topics, which will all lend themselves to educating a well-rounded individual. But that exposure can be confusing. You have any number of topics, all taught by (hopefully) enthusiastic professors. It is easy to be interested in psychology when you have a professor who is great at making each theory relevant. It is easy to get wrapped up in humanities when you have a professor who helps you feel the true essence of each society you study. Or an astronomy professor who opens up the universe to you. The list can go on indefinitely.

There are basically four types of students who enter college, with regard to majors:

1. The student who knows exactly what they want. This is pretty rare. From experience, this is likely to be someone who has known for a long time what they want to do (be a teacher, be a doctor, etc.).

2. The student whose parents have pretty much let them know what they are going to major in. Sometimes, this works out great. The more the student knows about the field, the more he or she likes it. Other times... The best outcome, of course, is for parents and students to both be happy. But in the end... the student has to live with the degree of choice and work in that field.

3. The student who has a general idea of what he or she might want to do. In this case, the student can select the closest major to his or her interests and change the major with very little problem later, if need be.

4. The student who doesn't have a clue what he or she wants to do. In this instance, most schools have a major designation for students who have not made up their minds yet. Chances are, this student will get interested in one of the basic classes over the first couple of years and want to know more about the topic. If this is you, keep in touch with your advisor. Odds are, they have been doing this for years and can help you navigate to a major more quickly.

Regardless of the major upon entering, many, if not most, students will want to change their major at some point. This is so very normal. If you decide you want to change, talk to your advisor about what that means with regard to additional classes, scholarship issues, etc. But please, don't stress about it. It will work out!

University and College Structure

"He who is afraid of asking
is ashamed of learning."
Danish Proverb

Universities are set up very differently than high schools. A university is like a mini-city. The people are in this city to assist you in your success. On most campuses you will find health services, safety officers, a bank, recreation, food venues, workout facilities, and depending on the nature of the campus, perhaps even spiritual services.

There is a President or Chancellor at the very top of the organizational structure. Then there are several Vice President/Chancellors. Several of the Vice Presidents/Chancellors are set in place to help the university itself function. Each Vice President/Chancellor is in charge of a division of the university. A university may have a Vice President for Information Technology, a Vice Chancellor for Multicultural Services, Vice President for Administration and Finance, etc. The two divisions that you will encounter the most are the two we will talk about here.

Division of Academic Affairs

Whether or not this is the exact term used at the university, this division is over all things related to the curriculum and the classroom. The people you will know best from this division are the faculty members, or your professors. Each professor belongs to a particular department (which is sometimes called a school). Your major will be in one of these departments. There are generally several majors in each department. One of the faculty members in the department will also be the Department Chair. This person's responsibility is to make sure the students taking classes from that department are learning everything they should be learning and to make sure that the faculty are getting their needs met too.

Often at a university, several departments are then grouped together. These departments form a college. There are generally several colleges. For example: You could have the College of Math and Sciences. Within that college are the Biology Department (Pre-Med majors, Zoology majors, etc.), Physics Department, Math Department, and more. At the head of each college is the Dean. This person oversees all of the departments, with the Department Chairs reporting to him or her. The Deans then report to the Vice President for Academic Affairs, also known as the Provost. This person looks at the big picture for the entire university, with respect to the classroom and learning.

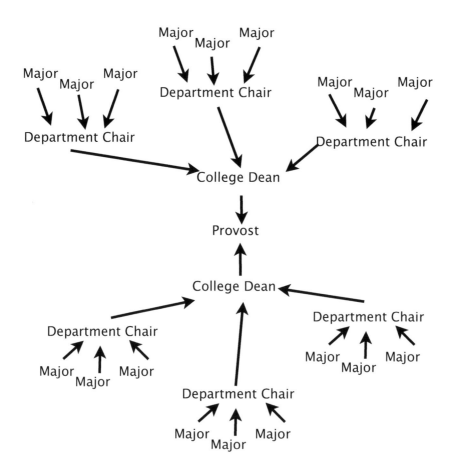

Division of Student Affairs (or Student Services)

The division of student affairs encompasses a variety of departments. It ensures a successful "out of class experience." Universities differ in which departments fall under this division. However, most will include: Campus Life or Campus Activities (student organizations, student government, Greek Life & events), Career Services (help you find internships and jobs), Health Center (doctors/nurses), Wellness/Fitness Center (gym), Multicultural Student Services (sometimes its own division within the university), International Office (international student services), Counseling Center, and Residential Life (housing).

The Division of Student Affairs has a Vice President (or Dean of Students) and the various department directors. The purpose of this division is to help you with everything outside of the classroom. They understand what you are going through and what you need to get through whatever your problem may be. Seek these people out. They are there for YOU.

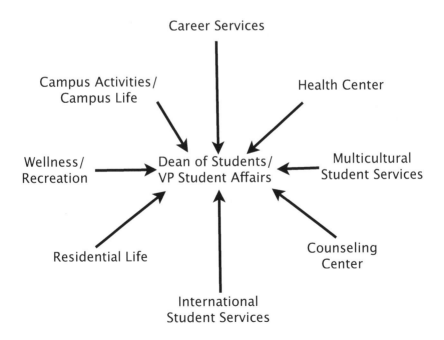

College Credit Hours

"The beautiful thing about learning is nobody can take it away from you."
B.B. King, Legendary blues guitarist

Similar to high school, college students will take several classes each semester. However, the credit received by college students is measured differently than those a high school student receives. College courses are generally broken down by the credit hour, sometimes just called credits or hours.

Each course taken in college is worth so many credit hours. Usually, the credit hours are determined by how many hours you spend in that course each week for the average length of a semester. So this may look different if you are taking a summer course. For example, a traditional course may be worth three credit hours which means that you attend the course three hours in one week (e.g. Monday, Wednesday, and Friday for one hour each day or Tuesday and Thursday for an hour and half each day).

The more credit hours per course the more time you spend in class that week, and fewer the credit hour per course the less time you spend in class that week. The exceptions are labs and studios. For your average class, you can figure you should be spending two hours outside of class, working on the class, for every one hour of credit. That's six hours of additional study time per week for a three hour class. Since lab and studio work must be done in a lab/studio, that additional time is made up in the lab. Students should also expect to spend the same amount of time working on an online course as they would any other course.

Grade Point Average (GPA)

Each course taken in college is given a completion grade. This grade is on an A-F scale for most normal courses. Your GPA is figured according to the number of hours you took and your grade. An "A" is worth 4 points, just as in high school, and so on. To figure your GPA, multiply the number of hours by the number of points from each grade.

The number of hours for a course is, for a many campuses, the last number of the course number (2713= 3 hours, 404= 4 hours -> the first number being the course level with Freshman level starting at 1000 or 100 and Senior level being 4000 or 400).

So for example, if you took 12 hours (4 classes at 3 hours each) and received the following grades: A (4pts X 3hrs= 12pts), B (3pts X 3hrs= 9pts), A (4pts X 3hrs= 12pts), C (2pts X 3hrs= 6pts). Your total points would be 39. Divide that by the number of hours (39/12) and you get your GPA (3.25).

If your college or university assigns grades with "+" or "-", the calculation process will be similar, though the numerical values for the grade may differ slightly. Your cumulative GPA is your GPA for all semesters combined.

Courses taken for a pass/fail credit are not added in the GPA. They are, however, added to the total number of course credits needed for graduation. Additionally, AP (Advanced Placement) courses, taken in high school can earn credit as well as CLEP testing (College Level Examination Program). If you know a topic extremely well, you can attempt to "test out" of it. If you pass the test, you do not have to take the actual class. AP and CLEP course will not be added into your GPA either.

1283	College Alegbra	A	(3 hrs X 4 pts) 12 pts
2343	Cognitive Psychology	B	(3 hrs X 3 pts) 9 pts
2723	Speech Communiction	A	(3 hrs X 4 pts) 12 pts
1473	Intro to Philosophy	C	(3 hrs X 2 pts) 6 pts
			39 pts
		Divided by	12 hrs
			3.25

Getting the Most Out of Class

"It must be remembered that the purpose of education is not to fill the minds of students with facts... it is to teach them to think."
Robert M. Hutchins (1899-1977),
Former president & chancellor of Univ of Chicago

Once you are in college and going to class, there is no need to make life harder than it has to be. You will want to maximize your efforts, most efficiently. Here are some tips to get you started.

❋ **Find how things connect**. One thing people who have graduated from college say they wish they had known when they started college is how connected everything is. You will take Humanities and learn about some of the same people you discussed in your Philosophy class and your Communication class. The same theories will pop up in several other classes as well. Don't study for classes in a vacuum. All subjects are related somehow. There is an interconnectedness of all things in life...and in college.

❋ **Find what works for you**. Get a system. Whether it is taking extensive notes, using a tape recorder, outlining the chapters or something entirely different-- you need to be sure that you figure out what meets your needs and learning style.

❋ **Go to class**. You are on your own now and have the option whether to show up or not. No one is going to call your parents if you don't show up. YOU are your own parent. Don't let yourself get swept into the stay-up-all-night, and then miss class routine. It is the fastest way to end your college career. Be sure to check your syllabus (aka your contract for the class) to find out about the attendance policy for each class. For example, if you miss too many days, you may automatically fail the course or be withdrawn from it. You have worked hard to get to this point; don't blow it by expecting someone else to take responsibility. It is up to you now. And you can do it.

✸ **Talk to your professors**. This is so very important and can make a major difference in your grades. Your professors are not in this position for the money; they are in it because they want to help you grow and become the wonderful and successful person you were meant to be. However, if you don't communicate with them, they have no way of knowing what is going on with you. If you are sick, stressed, need help with something…talk to them— they can help.

✸ **Learn how to learn**. It is such a waste to spend four years in college and come out "knowing it all." Why? Because "it all" changes. Constantly. Your college years should be a time to whet your appetite for discovery, exploration, and continuous improvement. It is a perfect opportunity to learn how be a student of life. Once you graduate, you either follow that path or become that stale person stuck in whatever decade you came of age in. Don't be that person. Discover the joys of life long learning!

✸ **Go to the library**. It is a resource haven, just waiting to welcome you in your quest for knowledge! Seriously though, learn to use the resources at the library and how to connect with the electronic resources at home. It can also provide a quiet, conducive environment for studying and rooms for study groups. Plus, many now have coffee shops!

✸ **Remember what you are in college for**. You are in college to study, to learn, to achieve. At the end of it all, you will have earned a degree. College is supposed to be a time for having fun and for learning who you are. Take time to make friends, exercise, get involved, be alone now and then, and to study. Keeping your life in balance while you are in college can be a difficult task, but is absolutely necessary to the overall well-being of YOU!

Study Abroad

One of the coolest opportunities you will have in college is to go somewhere else in the world and get credit for it. When you go to another country, your perspective on your own country and ways of thinking cannot help but to be altered. You see how others sleep and eat, how they communicate and fill their time. This changes the way we view life, forever. It is an education that literally opens up the world to you. Very few things you do in college will have such a profound effect on the rest of your life.

There are a few different ways to do this, but you need to start planning early.

※ Semester Abroad: Most schools have agreements with a variety of schools in other countries. They are basically exchange programs where students can enroll in the college oversees for a semester. You will earn credits that will count toward your degree and the tuition is pretty comparable, if not the exact same as your own school. However, costs associated with travel and entertainment need to be assessed and planned for. This is a junior or senior year adventure.

※ Short Courses Abroad: A variety of professors in all sorts of fields (at your college) likely make trips overseas with students for short courses "in the field." These usually last from a week to a month, but may be more depending on the nature of the field. They are likely to happen in the summer and will be intensive study in that country for credit.

※ Other opportunities: Other opportunities exist for you to work (perhaps teaching English as a second language), volunteering, or studying in another country.

Talk to your Study Abroad Office your Freshman year. They can guide you on the best opportunities for you, as well as the costs associated with each. Regardless of which you choose, it is worth saving your money and going. You will never regret it.

Unique 2U

Just fifteen years ago an online degree was pretty much a joke. Today, distance learning is thriving and is an essential part of most campuses. One way to stay balanced and stay current is to take an online course. Chances are your university has plenty to offer. There are also many other accredited schools out there from which to choose. As with any university, you can explore it's credibility by checking out the accreditation page, then going to that accreditation body's website and checking them out... See what other schools are listed. Are those reputable schools? Have you heard of any of them?

Online courses are not for everyone. Before you take one, you should know a few things:

* Though it may be more convenient, **do not mistake it for being easier**. Almost always you will find the courses as, if not more, challenging than standard classroom courses.

* You will **need to be more motivated, more self-driven**. You should first figure out how you work best. Since, for the majority of classes, there is no set time to meet, you must find time to go online and post your assignment, reply to discussion threads (you are graded on class participation), etc.

* You will be **expected to use the technology right away**. Your grade will depend on it. It may take you quite some time to figure out how to post assignments, where to go for discussions, etc. There may be some classes or workshops offered on your campus that can train you to use this technology. You will want to become familiar with it *before* you take an online class.

* You have many options today. **Be sure to discuss your them with your advisor**.

GETTING INVOLVED ON CAMPUS

"Don't be afraid to go out on a limb;
that's where the fruit is."
H. Jackson Brown, Author

The move from high school to college can make some students nervous. Not knowing many people, being away from your parents, and just getting used to "college life" are things that most freshmen encounter. But there are systems in place that can help you assimilate into college life. One of the quickest ways to meet new people and to get to know your new home is to join a student organization.

Types of Student Organizations

"I don't know who my grandfather was;
I am much more concerned to what his
grandson will be."
Abraham Lincoln (1809-1865),
16th President of the USA

Several different types of student organizations exist on a college campus. Finding one that is a good fit for your personality and time commitments is important. Student organizations are created and run by students, for students. This means that you cannot only join them, but you can create them as well. Keep that in mind if you get to college and find that there is a need for something that does not yet exist. All campuses have different organizations. There are some common ones and then there are unique ones. Here are some of the basic types of organizations common to most campuses.

Campus-wide organizations

☀ *Student government*. Student governments have an important role in college. The student government organization usually oversees almost all other student organizations. Each college is unique; however, there are some rather common aspects to most student governments. The three major executive positions at a school are, in general, the Student Body President, Vice President, and the Senate Chair. The President and Vice President are the executive branch, just like in big government. They will often meet with student body executives from other schools, state government officials, and the college administrators. They are the voices and the faces representing the students to these entities. On smaller campuses, some of these positions may be combined.

There is also a legislative branch, the senate. Student organizations and other student populations elect senators. These senators meet and discuss budgets, programming and on-campus changes they would like to recommend to the administration. Anyone interested in government or student government would do well to get involved with the senate at first. It is a great way to meet others who are involved and to make a difference on campus. You will have the opportunity, more than likely, to join several committees within the senate.

At schools where Student Activity Fees are assessed, the student government association is generally the one that gives out the funding from the fees to the student organizations.

> "When you do nothing, you feel overwhelmed and powerless. But when you get involved, you feel the sense of hope and accomplishment that comes from knowing you are working to make things better."
> Pauline R. Kezer, Former legislator & Connecticut political leader

☀ *Programming*. At most schools there is a student programming board of some kind. It may be a general campus organization or it could be housed with the student union. No matter where it is, these organizations have a lot going on. They will generally have one of the, if not the, largest budget of any student organization on campus. At larger schools, their advisor is likely to be a full time advisor. Programming board structures vary from college to college. There are, however, some events that are more common: late night weekend programming, concerts, casino/bingo nights, speakers, tailgate parties, tradition events, and more.

✵ **Campus traditions**. Homecoming, Annual Events, etc. - Traditions that are too large for a programming board will often be a student organization in and of themselves. Homecoming, for example, usually takes an entire year to plan. The same goes for other large campus tradition events. These boards are formed with only one goal/event in mind.

Professional student organizations

Just about every major has a corresponding student organization. These organizations allow you to get to know other people in your same major and to begin networking with people in your field. The organizations will generally meet on a regular basis and have some traditions and/or events. Professors in the field serve as the advisors. Getting to know your classmates and your professors, plus more about your field, will only help you in the long run!

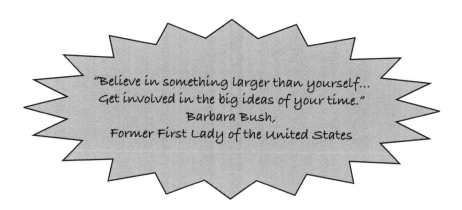

"Believe in something larger than yourself...
Get involved in the big ideas of your time."
Barbara Bush,
Former First Lady of the United States

Special interest organizations

✻ *Greek Organizations*. Fraternities and Sororities on most campuses hold recruitment or "Rush." Traditionally, Interfraternity Council (men) and Panhellenic (women) host a "Rush Week" at the start of the fall and spring semesters as a way to select new members. During this "Rush Week," events are held by all of the different Interfraternity Council fraternities and by the Panhellenic sororities as a way to show the potential members a little bit of what each chapter is about. At the end of the week, students are allowed to join any house that wants to sign them.

Pan-Hellenic organizations', which are the historically African-American fraternities and sororities (not to be confused with Panhellenic – which, though both Greek, governs a different set of organizations), and other multicultural fraternities and sororities, have a different process for those who are interested in membership. These organizations are usually open for membership after a student has acquired some college hours. The amount of hours needed to join an organization varies depending on the organization's national regulations. When these organizations are preparing for a group to enter their organization, there will be flyers placed on campus and in campus newspapers announcing the organization's "Rush." It is at the "Rush" that the interested student will learn the specific qualifications and procedures to become a member of the organization.

Choosing which fraternity or sorority to join is a very important decision. While you can change your mind and decide not be active in the organization, it is best to find the right organization for you at the start.

After you choose the fraternity or sorority you would like to join, your path will differ depending on which organization you are interested in. Most Pan-Hellenic fraternities and sororities will have an "intake" period, where you are informed on the responsibilities of being a member, the history of the organization, and the organizations main philanthropic focuses. Interfraternity Council and Panhellenic will have a "pledge" period, where you get a limited view of what being a member is like, and you also will learn more about the history of the organization. Think of your pledgeship as joining the organization on a "trial-basis." While you will get more privileges as a full member, it will definitely give you an idea of what you are joining. After the pledge period, many organizations have some form of initiation or ceremony, which will make you an actual member of the group.

To make your decision of which chapter to join easier, you should ask questions during recruitment. Ask someone in the chapter about dues. Dues for Interfraternity and Panhellenic organizations are monthly fees paid by both members and pledges. The exact amount will vary from college to college and house to house. For Pan-Hellenic organizations, dues are usually an annual event. All Greek chapter dues usually go partly to the local chapter and to the National Headquarters.

Another key factor when choosing an organization is to look at what the chapters have done and decide which are most important to you. Ask about their grades, campus and community involvement, athletics, etc. Try to find an organization that shares similar goals with you.

You can visit the internet and determine what the organization represents nationally. Many times, once you have joined these organizations you will be active in them after college as well, so you want to make sure that you would be proud of your choice for a lifetime.

In order to get the most out of "Going Greek," follow this simple bit of advice: Pick the organization where you feel the most comfortable.

Hazing is illegal in every state and in every house/chapter. The definition of hazing is: an act which recklessly or intentionally endangers the mental or physical health or safety of a student, or which destroys or removes public or private property, for the purpose of initiation, admission into, affiliation with, or as a condition for continued membership in, a group or organization. Though this can be interpreted many ways, there are two principles to keep in mind always.

→ 1. If it makes you or someone else uncomfortable, mentally or physically, don't do it and don't ask others to do it.

→ 2. What may seem harmless in your class has a tendency to be one-up'ed in the next class. With this snowball effect, within just a couple of years, students could be put in real danger. It is best not to start that process at all.

✳ *Multicultural and International Organizations* - There is so much to be said about becoming a member of a multicultural organization. The support received from peers who share the same background, ethnicity and culture can be extremely valuable. Whatever background you relate to, there is a group that meets your interest (and if there is not, start one). Becoming a member of an organization is fairly easily. Usually at the start of the semester, organizations are eager for enthusiastic new members and this would be your opportunity to join. You can find information about the time and dates of the meetings through the Campus Life/Campus Activities department, by flyers, online communities (i.e. facebook), the school newspaper or by a student organization fair.

> "If you're not actively involved in getting what you want, you don't really want it."
> Peter McWilliams (1949-2000),
> Writer & publisher of self-help books

✳ *Religious, Lifestyles, Hobbies, etc.*- In addition to the types of organizations we've already discussed, campuses offer opportunities that meet a variety of other needs and interests. There are usually religious organizations that represent every major religion at the school, as well as LGBTQ orgs and orgs for sports (fencing, soccer, etc.), hobbies (movie watchers, rock climbing, rifle teams, etc.), political organizations (College Republicans, Young Democrats, etc.) and pretty much anything else that people would want to come together to do or discuss. These organizations are here to help you find your campus family and will introduce you to people with similar interests.

✺ *Volunteer/Community Service*- Another way to get involved is to volunteer in the community. Most larger (and quite a few smaller) campuses have a Volunteer Center or Volunteer Coordinator. This person's job is to serve as a clearinghouse of community projects and community agencies for the campus. Volunteering is a great way to meet people and make the community a better place. There are a variety of ways to serve.

✺ You can volunteer to work at an agency or to do a community-requested project.

✺ You can also get involved with large-scale campus-wide community service events (Big Event, Heart Walk, Relay for Life). The community service events are many times organized like a student organization, with an executive team and committees.

✺ Join a service organization (Rotaract, Colleges Against Cancer)

✺ Some of your courses in college may have you do a service learning project. Service learning is a term used when referring to doing something in the community, relating to the topic of the course, that allows the student to apply the knowledge from the classroom or to gain knowledge on the topic that could not otherwise be learned as well in a classroom setting.

"Volunteer activities can foster enormous leadership skills. The non professional volunteer world is a laboratory for self-realization."
Mae West (1893-1980),
Actress & playwright

Student Organization Structures

Advisors

All student organizations have advisors/sponsors, who are faculty or staff members at the university or college. They are there to help you and your organization. Advisors generally volunteer to do this in addition to their regular jobs. They are adults who want to help and to be there for you. If you have questions about procedures or problems with anyone, they can be a great resource. Even if your question or problem doesn't have anything to do with the student organization, these people are there for you.

Advisors also help your organization follow the rules and have consistency over the years. Members change yearly, but your advisor may know more of the history (what has worked in the past and what has not worked). Every campus also has regulations that student organizations must follow (like where you can and cannot spend money, campus life meetings you must attend, etc.). Your advisor should know these rules (and if not, he or she will know how to find out).

Executive members

The "exec" team has a lot of responsibility. Consequently, these positions generally require more of a time commitment than other positions. Students normally work their way to this point by proving themselves first. Though each organization is unique, some common executive positions are: President, Vice-President, Treasurer, Secretary, Membership Coordinator, Marketing/PR/ Publicity, Committee Chair, and Senator. Each one of these positions requires special talents to be done well. I've never known a student who would not have done well in at least one of these positions, given the proper training and committment.

Committee member or Volunteer

This is where it begins. If you know which committee you would like to be on, or at least explore, then you can join it. If you are really not sure where you would be best suited, perhaps volunteering to help at events will give you more of an idea. College is a time to try on different hats. You might even try an organization/position you never thought you would be good at. By doing this, you may just find a hidden talent of yours.

Applying to Student Organizations

Organizations have different ways in which one becomes a member. In some cases, by simply attending the meetings, you are a member. In other organizations, you will need to submit an application, resume, and possibly do an interview. Never fear, help is here! Here are some tips to help you succeed at getting the position you want. Keep in mind that, as with most things in life, you will get better the more you practice. Don't worry if you don't get the first position you apply for. Use that opportunity as a learning experience.

Resumes

First, do some searching and find a format that you are comfortable with. Then, get busy writing it. Your resume is not the same as an application. Your resume should show that you are qualified for the position or at least have the potential to do well. Be sure to use a simple, easy to read font and leave enough white space so it doesn't look cluttered. Here is an example with some tips:

Your Name Here
1234 Address
(555) 555-5555
Email@emailme.com

Objective: Clearly state the position for which you are applying and why you would like that position. You want to state it in such a way as to show the reader that this position is a natural fit for you, so tie in some of your major qualification. But keep this to one to two sentences.

Education

Coursework for Bachelor of Arts Coursework, Foreign Languages

ABC College, Super City, ST   Expected Graduation: 5/2018
Concentration in Russian, Spanish, French, & Italian; 3.8 G.P.A.

Somewhere High School (You can keep the high school in there until you graduate from college– then drop it.)
Super City, ST   Graduated: 5/2014

Career History and Accomplishments

Title, Company   2012-2014
· Use action terms and as many bullets as you need in order to describe your responsibilities and accomplishments on this job.

· Worked, held, served, initiated, established, assisted, negotiated, founded- are all good examples of words to start your bullet points. No need to write a complete sentence- just the action you did for the company

· Start with your most recent position.

Title, Company   2011-2012
· You don't have to list every odd job you've ever had, just the major ones.

Memberships and Affiliations

· Treasurer, Student Council, Somewhere High School, 2013-2014
· Member, French Club, Somewhere High School, 2011-2014
· Use the organizations to which you belonged while in high school only until you have some from college to put on your resume. As your college activities grow- take out the high school stuff.

> "A ship in a harbor is safe but that is not what ships were built for."
> John A. Shedd (1859-?),
> Author & professor

Interviews

✻ **Dress for success**. Do NOT assume that just because you are interviewing for a college organization position, your appearance doesn't count- it does.

✻ **Research**. Organizations are ALWAYS impressed when you know about what they have done, their goals, etc. Look up websites, talk to others, go to the events.

✻ **Prepare**. Practice answering some possible questions, get a good night's sleep, eat a good breakfast.

✻ **Be on time**. In fact, be early. Being late shows that this organization is not a priority for you.

✻ **Make eye contact with everyone**. Try not to dart your eyes, but DO give everyone some time with your eyes. This communicates sincerity.

✻ **Be specific and honest with your answers**. Do NOT pretend you are something you are not. The organization is more than likely looking for certain qualities for specific positions. If you don't have those particular qualities, not only will they be disappointed, but you will probably not like the position either.

✳ ***Ask questions***. The more you know about the organization, chances are the more questions you will be able to ask. Inquire about their goals, how they accomplished something, how something is structured and certainly the time commitments involved. The answers will give you more of a feel for the organization. Remember: YOU are the interviewee AND an interviewer! If you go into the interview with that in mind, it will be easier. Are you the right person for this position? Is this the right position for you?

✳ ***Be polite***. Remember to say, "please" and "thank you," when appropriate.

✳ ***Be yourself***. Relax and just be who you are. Let your unique personality come out. They are not looking for a cookie-cutter person. They are looking for a real, genuine and unique person.

✳ ***Silly questions*** such as, "If you were ice cream, what flavor would you be?," are meant to see how quickly you think on your feet. There are no right or wrong answers, so just give it your best.

✳ ***Know where to go from here***- When will you know about the position?- Find out before you leave. Sending a thank you note is fine (especially if it will be a week or more before you will know something). Do NOT call them every day until you find out. Bugging them may hurt your chances.

✳ **Smile!!!!**

Networking/Making Connections

Never underestimate the power of making connections. You are not born knowing everyone you need to know. You must go meet them. Even if you aren't the most outgoing person in the world- networking does NOT have to be difficult. Some easy ways to meet new people:

- ❈ *Just show up to an organizational meeting.* Most organizations have open or general meetings and advertise them as such. For the most part, you don't even have to strike up the initial conversations. Organizations are so happy to have new faces; they will more than likely just start talking to you. Voila! Instant friends! Your new acquaintances can help you get to know others and other organizations.

- ❈ *Talk to people in your classes*. Start a study group. Ask them questions about getting involved.

- ❈ *Attend events*. Even if you are shy and don't say much, people will notice if you attend events on a regular basis. I've seen students show up to Coffee Houses regularly and eventually be asked to join the organization.

- ❈ *Online Communities*. Befriend those with similar interests. See what they're involved in.

You need to know that you are wanted by these organizations. They are looking for students that want to give to the school. If you are willing to work hard, learn from others and take on responsibility- you should have no trouble getting involved.

Time Management

Getting involved on campus means that your time will be quickly filled with planning and events. Here are some tips so you can make the grades you want and still have the out-of-class experience.

Why don't people manage their time? In general, one of these five ideas apply:

✺ They don't know how.

✺ They are too lazy to plan.

✺ They enjoy the adrenaline buzz of meeting tight deadlines and crisis management.

✺ Their lives are too full of time wasters to even think about it.

✺ They have tried before and didn't stick to it.

> "Until you value yourself,
> you won't value your time.
> Until you value your time,
> you will not do
> anything with it."
> M. Scott Peck (1936-2005),
> Psychiatrist and author

> "In all our deeds, the proper value
> and respect for time
> determines success or failure."
> Malcolm X (1925-1965),
> Muslim minister & human rights activist

Time Wasters

✺ **Indecision**. Think about it, worry about it, put it off, think about it, worry about it, etc.

✺ **Inefficiency**. Jumping in & implementing instead analyzing & designing first, poor organization, unproductive meetings.

✺ **Unanticipated interruptions**. Only having 'just enough time' doesn't allow for that call from Grandma you have to take or the milk jug that fell, exploded and covered everything in your kitchen with milk.

✺ **Procrastination**. Waiting until the last minute or failing to get things done in a timely manner.

✺ **Unrealistic time estimates**. Thinking you can get an extensive project done quickly.

✺ **Unnecessary errors**. This is often due to being too tired or eating too much junk food.

✺ **Crisis management**. Constantly solving problems in a time crunch (ink goes out and paper is due in one hour, etc.)

✺ **Technology**. Gaming, social networking, txting, phones.

✺ **Poor planning**. Not being proactive.

✺ **Failure to delegate**. Not allowing others perform and grow.

✺ **Lack of priorities**. If you don't put to do items in an order of importance, things that are less important may suck up too much for your time.

Time Savers

❋ **Budget your time wisely**. Keep a calendar and "To Do" lists, write everything down as soon as you hear about it– look at it often, plan ahead, establish personal deadlines, set aside time for reflection, set aside time for just having a good time.

❋ **Say "No" sometimes.** People may not like it, but it is your time and energy here, not theirs.

❋ **Ask for help.** If you don't know how (or why or when) find someone who does and ask.

❋ **Procrastinate as little as possible.** Do as much as you can as soon as you can do it.

❋ **Always keep your goals in mind.** This will help you push through and stay focused.

❋ **Ensure all meetings have a purpose**. Also a time limit, including only essential people– Do not waste other people's time.

❋ **Identify time vacuums**. What is sucking up your time?

❋ **Delegate.** It helps you and empower others.

❋ **Keep things simple**. Beware of small, less important details that can suck up lots of time.

❋ **Adjust priorities** as a result of new tasks/information.

❋ **Get enough sleep and eat more fresh/healthy foods** (Seriously.)

"Know the true value of time; snatch, seize and enjoy every moment of it. No idleness, no laziness, no procrastination; never put off till to-morrow what you can do to-day."
Lord Chesterfield (1694-1773),
British statesman

LEADING A TEAM

Leading a team can be one of the most challenging experiences of your life and one of the most rewarding. A team that works well together can take the organization or event to the next level. So much goes into leading a team. This chapter has some tips and tools that might come in handy.

> "We must remember that one determined person can make a significant difference, and that a small group of determined people can change the course of history."
> Sonia Johnson, Equal rights activist & writer

Traditions

Nearly any organization to which you will belong has traditions. Below are some of the various types found in schools, companies, clubs, etc. [8]

✺ *Ethics*. Organizations generally have tendencies, as a collective group, to be ethical or not so ethical. This comes out in work ethic (how much effort is put into projects), conversation (whether it be gossip, rumors or positives about others), jokes (are they for all to enjoy or can certain people not hear them without being offended), and general politeness (are members ordered around or do execs say please).

✺ *Events*. This can be anything from weekly meetings to monthly get-togethers to annual banquets. Organizations are sometimes known in the community through their events.

☀ *Rites of Passage*. People usually don't start out as the president of an organization. Celebrated steps of levels of participation (1 year mark, achieving a certain goal, etc.) are outward signs of accomplishments.

☀ *Stories and Heroes*. Clubs often have stories of greatness. "We had a guy once who sold 300 tickets to our event in just 2 days." These serve as great motivators that the organization is worthwhile and that we must all strive to be our best in it.

☀ *Superstitions*. Some organizations have certain "taboos" that no one is allowed to say or do or else "bad luck will fall on them." This serves to unify the members and create a certain uniqueness for the group. It also tends to raise awareness and involvement as well. For example, it is considered unlucky in the theatre to say the word "MacBeth" (unless you are doing the actual play of course).

☀ *Symbols*. Most organizations have a symbol or a logo to represent them.

"People support what they help create."
Unknown

Team Roles and Personalities

> "Do not worry about holding high position; worry rather about playing your proper role."
> Confucius

It takes all kinds of people for a team to function well. Not everyone is good at everything. *Team Task Masters* include the types of personalities there to get the job done. *Team Builders and Maintainers* include those wanting to establish and keep interpersonal relationships among group members. Self-centered members do nothing productive and are, most of the time, counter-productive. As a leader, be sure you have a good balance of task roles and maintenance roles, while keeping the self-centered ones to a minimum. Here are a few of the traits one might find for each of the team personalities listed. [9]

Team Task Masters

* ❋ **Initiates.** New ideas, goals, procedures, methods, and solutions.

* ❋ **Seeks and gives information.** Asks for/offers facts, details and suggestions, opinions, personal experience, and evidence relevant to the topic.

* ❋ **Clarifies**. Elaborates on ideas of others; gives examples, explanations; integrates facts, ideas and suggestions; clarifies purpose and goals; defines positions; and summarizes progress.

* ❋ **Energizes**. Stimulates activity and gets the group going on the right track.

* ❋ **Takes notes/minutes.** Serves as the group's "memory" by taking down all necessary information.

Team Builders and Maintainers

❋ **Supports**. Praises, agrees, and goes along with others.

❋ **Harmonizes**. Mediates, reconciles, and conciliates among other members.

❋ **Relieves tension.** Jokes with, relaxes, and reduces tension with other members.

❋ **Seeks opinions.** Draws out convictions, opinions, and values of others.

Self-Centered Members (don't be this person)

❋ **Blocks.** Constantly raises objections, insisting nothing will work or brings up old topics already rejected.

❋ **Is aggressive.** Jokes at the expense of others, deflates the status of others.

❋ **Seeks recognition.** Boasts, calls attention to self, relates irrelevant personal experiences, uses group to talk about personal mistakes, etc.

❋ **Clowns around.** Makes jokes in a cynical way, acts uninvolved with group processes.

❋ **Dominates**. Tries to take over the group by interrupting, ordering, etc.

Tuckman's Small Group Stages

Whether it's a group of people in an organization, college roommates, or just a group of friends, nearly every group goes through certain stages when it first begins. To know this won't necessarily stop it from happening, but it will give you a clue about how to deal with it. When you know what to do, you and your team can get through the hard times faster.

People are unique. When they come together, they are all bringing their own personalities, experiences, and dreams. These stages do not always occur just as they are written here. In fact, you may join some groups that seem to have no storms. But the storms actually help us grow stronger as a team. [10]

Forming

When a group first forms, the members are usually excited. "We're going to be the best team ever!" or "We have our own place now and we can do whatever we want!" This stage is fun and there is usually quite a bit of bonding, figuring out the *commonalities* between members, etc.

Storming

Here is the stage where we start to see the flaws: the person who always seems to be ten minutes late, or the one that "oops" forgot to do his/her part. The most wonderful roommate ever starts eating your food or leaving cabinet doors open. All of a sudden, we start seeing the faults and quirks in others. People start settling into their roles and members start seeing the *differences* between each other. This is not a fun stage. There is usually tension and perhaps unkind words. When this happens, don't despair…

Norming

There is a ray of sunshine peeking through the clouds; the storm is almost over. We start getting used to some of the little quirks. "Oh, that's just him/her." Some of the habits may not be acceptable at all. That is when the group must start making rules for themselves. They must also make some agreed-upon consequences if the rules are not followed. Eventually, what we can live with becomes "normal" and what we can't live with is corrected. We level out.

Performing

Now that everyone is okay with everyone again, the group can begin, finally, to accomplish something or to live happily.

> "Never doubt that a small group of thoughtful, committed citizens can change the world; indeed, it's the only thing that ever has."
> Margaret Mead (1901-1978),
> Cultural anthropologist

Be Careful

Especially today, with all of the instant and constant communication, it is very easy to slip into a habit of discussing frustrations about a certain person with other members of the group, collectively or one-on-one. A great leader wants his or her members to all be successful and does everything he or she can to help them. This does not include chatting about them behind their backs. Wiser to stay professional, go through the Norming stage and save the "OMG's" for that really ridiculous commercial you just saw- jk... (But not about the norming.)

Management of Tools & Resources

When you are leading a team, there are so many important things to consider. Leadership concerns the influence you have on your team and getting your team to follow you to the goal. Management, on the other hand, is about the responsibilities of getting the job done. There are some who make good managers but are not the best leaders and there are others who make wonderful leaders, but are not so great at management.

Should you become an exec of an organization, like a president, you will need the leadership skills to get everyone on board. You will also need management skills to accomplish your tasks. Here are some of the resources you will want to stay on top of.

> "The best executive is the one who has sense enough
> to pick good men [and women] to do
> what he [or she] wants done,
> and self-restraint enough to keep
> from meddling with them while they do it."
> Theodore Roosevelt (1858-1919),
> 26th President of the United States

Time

Planning ahead and organizing the time you have is critical. When you first take on a project, create a timeline. This will include all of the steps necessary for getting the job done on time. Set deadlines and assign group members to specific tasks. Everyone does better when they know what to do and when to do it.

Budget

Remember that almost everything will cost something. Don't spend first and count later... Make a budget, checking prices before you begin to spend any money. Projects generally take more money than we think. Often, a couple of extra expenses that no one thinks of in the beginning will pop up at some point. Be sure to plan for them. Keep track of everything you spend, what you spend it on, and how you paid for it.

People

The management of people can be very different than leading them. Leadership is about inspiration, motivation, and commitement. It is working from the inside out. In a managerial perspective, people are your most important resource. Without your team, there is only you to do it all. Check out your team and who is on it. What would each person do best? Assigning people the right tasks not only keeps them satisfied with the group, but helps to get the job done most efficiently and effectively too. Success is being both a great manager and an inspiring leader.

"Of all the things I've done, the most vital is coordinating the talents of those who work for us and pointing them towards a certain goal."
Walt Disney (1901-1966),
Film producer & entrepreneur

Goals

Do NOT begin your projects without a goal. You will have no idea if you've gotten there if you don't know where you are going. Your team will function more effectively if they know what it is that they are working towards. This will help members stay on track and focused.

Information

This one may not be as obvious as some of the others. What you tell your team, how you tell them and when you tell them, really makes a difference. Your team needs to know the goals and the plan, for sure. But sometimes too much information hurts the cause. If someone is working on a particular area of a project, he or she, for example, does not necessarily need to know all about the issues in a completely different area. Bogging down team members' brains is not a good practice and can simply be overwhelming.

Some information needs to be shared, but also needs the right timing. Waiting until the right moment can mean everything. As a manager, you have access to information that others do not. You don't want to hold back critical information or compliments from the team. You might, however, want to hold back on non-critical issues and issues involving others. If your team does not trust that you can hold your tongue when you need to, they will be less likely to share critical information with you.

Inventory

Resources, of course, include supplies. Your team will function more effectively and efficiently if they have the necessary supplies to do their jobs. Be sure to include equipment needs in your budget. It is easy to forget about materials before you get started, but impossible to forget about them after the project is underway. Try to plan ahead. If this is not your area of strength, ask one of your task masters to help you.

> "The project manager is expected to integrate all aspects of the project, ensure that the proper knowledge and resources are available when and where needed, and above all, ensure that the expected results are produced in a timely, cost-effective manner."
> Jack R. Meredith & Samuel J. Mantel, Authors

> "There are basically two types of people. People who accomplish things, and people who claim to have accomplished things. The first group is less crowded."
> Mark Twain (1835-1910),
> Author & humorist

Meetings

You, of course, will want to hold meetings if you are leading a team. It is a wonderful way to make sure that everyone is communicating with one another and staying on the same page. Some of the major reasons teams meet are:

※ Regularly scheduled

※ Problem solving

※ Exchanging information

※ Planning

※ Training

Holding a meeting is more than just getting together to talk about "stuff." Some of the reasons *why meetings fail* (and/or don't get anything accomplished) are:

※ People don't care enough

※ Too many self-centered people

※ Conflict within the group/ negative attitudes

※ People are at the meeting that don't need to be

※ No agenda

There are some things you can do to make sure that you are not conducting fruitless meetings. Your time is valuable and the more you can accomplish at the meeting, the more time you have to get "stuff" done.

Agenda

Don't leave home without it! Set a schedule of items you want to cover and know what you need to bring before you go into the meeting. Identify the goals you have for the meeting, who needs to be there and how long the meeting should take. You may want to email the agenda to those who will be attending, prior to the meeting- so they too can be prepared.

Tone

It is up to the leader to set the tone of the meeting. Be open to what others are saying and they too will be open. Speak in a positive way towards the goal and they too will be positive. If possible, have some refreshments there...people love food! Making the experience enjoyable will help members feel comfortable and want to be there.

Focus

When you are in the meeting, stay on target. This does not mean that you can't have fun. It does mean that you don't want to waste everyone's time. People will begin to dread meetings when nothing is accomplished. Stick to the agenda, as best you can. Also, try to use as few words as possible to get your point across. Don't be the person who feels the need to drone on and on and on and on and on... long after everyone has stopped listening. It is better to leave them wanting more and asking you a few questions.

Assignments

Make sure you have been clear on who is doing what. If you would like members to give updates, be sure they know this before the meeting. Some people hate to be put on the spot (others may not mind- but you want to consider everyone). Also, if you want someone to take minutes (aka note taking), be sure they are aware of this ahead of time.

Where to go from here

Do NOT forget this step. Everyone should walk away from the meeting knowing what he or she is supposed to do before the next meeting. If a next step is not discussed, chances are, it will not get done until you have another meeting about what to do next. It is best to do it all in the same meeting. In addition, you will want to set the next meeting date and time if possible. Be sure everyone knows what to do and when to have it done.

Unique 2U

No other generation has had the ability to communicate as you do. We have everything to save time and yet, we have less of it then we ever have. To save time, you may want to utilize some of the other communication tools available. "Reply All" email meetings work for quick updates. Texting and messaging work for person-to-person communications. Face-to-face meetings are still the best way to be sure everyone is on the same page and to clarify details. However, phone and/or video conferencing are great options if a member or two can't physically make it to the meeting.

> "When spider webs unite, they can tie up a lion."
> Ethiopian Proverb

ALL ABOUT EVENTS

"If I were invited to a
dinner party with my
characters,
I wouldn't show up."
Dr. Seuss (1904-1991),
Writer, poet & cartoonist

Coordinating events is a major aspect of many organizations. Whether it's a Student Council fundraiser or your work place holiday party, nearly every group has functions. We will explore event planning– what to do and when to do it. This is just a general overview, so your specific events may include more or less than what is listed here. No matter how large or small the function, though, the key is planning ahead. We will first explore some common types of events (and a little about each type). Then we will go through the planning process and discuss some important items related to nearly all events.

Types of Events

Reception

These are usually held:

✻ Immediately before another event (ex: before a banquet)

✻ Immediately after another event (ex: after a wedding)

✻ To kick off a series of events (ex: beginning of Greek Week)

✻ To honor a person/persons/etc. (ex: retirement or awards ceremony)

✻ To gather a group of people for socialization and/or a meet and greet.

Receptions are generally a less expensive way to gather many people to celebrate something, especially when you are not quite sure how many people will be attending. It is appropriate to have some light foods and something to drink. Depending on the occasion, the audience, and your budget, you may have cookies and punch or little sandwiches, cheese and cracker platters, coffee, water or perhaps something that is unique to the event and goes with the theme.

The way you set up the room will depend on the situation. If the point of the reception is simply to watch a short program, then standing room only is fine. If the program is going to be a little longer, having rows of chairs where people will eventually sit (after they get their refreshments and mingle a little) is good. If there is to be no real program and you want people to be able to talk and get to know each other and to stay a little while, having tables (round ones) with (or tall tables without) chairs is a good idea. – It is appropriate to put on the invitation that there will be a program (and when you plan to start it), if you are having one. If you want to hold a simple "meet and greet", you can just say when the reception begins and ends. Proper etiquette at a reception:

"Proper prior planning prevents pitifully poor performance."
unknown

❀ DO feel free to make a small plate.

❀ Do NOT overload the plate or heap it. This is not intended to be a meal. If you are really hungry and feel you need a large plate, it is better to go back a couple of times.

❀ DO take a napkin and use any forks, picks, etc. that are available (as opposed to using your fingers– if possible). Many receptions are set up so that people can visit one another; you will want to have a clean hand to shake with.

❀ Do NOT continue to talk when a program is going on. Even if you meet the most interesting person ever, finish the conversation after the program.

❀ DO meet new people and say hello to those you already know. If nothing else, you can comment on how good (or bad) the food is.

Banquet/Dinner

There are numerous reasons to hold banquets or dinners (too numerous to really list). They do usually signify a more important event (such as a major annual event) than a reception; however, that is not always the case.

A normal banquet table seats 8-10 people (depending on the size of the table). Table designations are an important item to think about. You can choose to either have open seating (in which case you will want to reserve one or more tables at the front for VIPs) or assigned seating. Banquets/dinners that people pay for (more than $10-ish), usually have assigned seating. This is so that people who purchase seats together can sit together. Quite a few people, though, will come as single persons or as a couple. So, you will need to place them at a table. When designating the seating, it is really important to consider your attendees and what they would want. If you know, for example that someone is really into a particular hobby and someone else shares that interest, put them at the same table. If, on the other hand, you know that there is a potential clash in interests or beliefs, place those people at different tables. You want people to strike up conversations and enjoy themselves, not argue. Treat everyone as an honored guest.

Proper etiquette at a banquet or dinner:

✸ DO talk to the people at your table. Asking them questions about what they do, what their majors are, etc. are great ways to open the conversation.

✸ DO start on your salad when everyone is seated at your table and at least most of the room is seated. You will probably have a set table of water (and perhaps tea), and a salad (and possibly a dessert) when you get there. You may drink the water (and/or tea) whenever you want. Your forks are placed in the order in which you will use them (if you have one above your plate, it is for dessert). Start with the outside (left) fork and eat your salad. Cut any pieces larger than bite sized. Don't cram a giant piece of lettuce in your mouth. Leave your fork on your plate when you are finished (some people turn the fork upside down to indicate to the wait staff that they are finished).

✻ Do NOT start eating your meal until everyone at your table has been served a meal. The table starts eating together. Use your next fork in. If there is something on the plate that you don't like, don't talk about it– just don't eat it. Eat what you like from the plate.

✻ DO use your manners. Ask others to "please pass…" something that is not directly in front of you. Chew with your mouth closed. Cut food into manageable bites, etc.

✻ DO enjoy the experience.

✻ The default dress code is a suit or a nice cocktail dress.

Luncheon

In many ways this may resemble the dinner/banquet above. However, luncheons are usually less formal. In fact, many luncheons are buffet or brown bag style. They are generally shorter in length than the dinner because people have jobs/ classes/sessions to attend after the luncheon. The seating is usually more open than at a dinner and the program starts sooner into the meal. Sandwiches, salads or "light" meals are appropriate for a luncheon. The default dress code is business attire.

Dance/Recreation

Dances can be formal or more of a party-type style. If it is formal, be sure it is indicated on the invitations. Recreational events are events where the attendees actually participate in something (besides eating). Examples of recreational events: BINGO nights, craft-making, game show-type events, sports, etc. Fairly unique to dances and recreational events:

✻ Prizes. Whether they are door prizes or prizes for the best something or other, you will want them to be something desirable to your attendees. Prizes should match the feel of your event. If the event is casual, the prizes do not need to be wrapped or in bags. They can just be there. The more formal the event, the more formal the presentation of the prize should be. For example, if you purchased (or had donated) an item with your school logo on it, you might put the item in a basket and wrap it with some colored cellophane to dress it up.

✳ Supplies: Be sure that you have planned for all the supplies you will need. Do NOT forget to consider: tape, scissors, paper, glue, or anything else you may need to make something, hang something, or fix something last minute.

✳ Also somewhat unique to these events: Security. Depending on how many people (and the audience) you expect, you should consider whether or not you want security. Your security may be accomplished by having chaperones or you may want to hire a security officer. Just remember that you want your attendees to be and feel safe. By just having these people present, you will be discouraging students from doing anything stupid or disruptive.

Concert/Speaker

There is quite a bit about this under the programming section later in the chapter. However, here we will discuss some items unique and very important to this type of event. When planning a large event such as this type, you may be working with an agent. If you are, you MUST discuss all major wishes and changes with them. Discuss with agent and/or performer:

✳ The agenda of the program. Do you want this person(s) to come to a special dinner before the program? A VIP reception before or after? A book signing? An autograph signing? If so, be ready to tell them what time you would like to do this, how long it will last, how many people (as in the dinner) will be attending, who will be escorting the guest to and from these events, etc. Once approved, ANY changes (time, location, people involved) should be cleared with the agent/performer. You may not think that a half an hour change makes much difference, but it may to the performer.

✻ Any opening acts/bands/other speakers/etc. A performer/speaker has an image. If they are to continue to build a name/keep a name for themselves, they must protect that image. Therefore, it is their right to make the ultimate decision about who/what will be associated with them. Some performers/speakers are very easy-going, while others are very particular about the events.

✻ Concert contracts should come with a "Rider." This is basically everything that the artist/band wants/needs. It should include technical equipment, stage size/needs, food/beverage desires, etc. Before the contract is signed, be sure that you have checked out all of the items in the rider. Can you pay for them? Can you find/provide them, given your own geographical area? Be honest about the items with the agent. Once the contract is signed, you are legally bound to it and will be expected to provide the items.

Some hints: If you are not allowed (legally) to purchase meals with the funds you have, ask if you can increase the overall fee of the performer so he or she can buy meals (same goes with travel requirements). If the technical needs are more than what you have, call companies that provide the service and equipment and ask them for quotes. Be sure to check with your advisor on the proper procedures for contracts.

Workshops

Workshops are held to teach or train people how to do something or to educate them on a concept. One key factor to remember is that in a workshop the attendees should participate. If they are simply listening to a speaker in order to learn, it is called a seminar. When one comes to a workshop, one expects to be doing something.

If you are having a workshop with many people, you will probably want to break them up into groups (how you divide them is up to you). The ideal group size is 5-7 people. Depending on what you are asking them to do, you may want to increase or decrease that number.

If you hold a workshop to train, be sure to have enough of the necessary supplies or tools for everyone to participate. It's okay to ask participants to share or to do something together, just make certain that you have enough supplies so that everyone can do something.

If you are holding a workshop to learn about a concept, you will probably have them discuss something, decide something, etc. That being the case, you will want to have instructions and/or questions at each station (with each small group). Having a facilitator (or designating a group member to be one) can really help keep the group on track.

Keep in mind: People can only hold their focus on something or sit still for a limited amount of time. Breaks, energizers, and food really help to keep your attendees focused and learning while in sessions. If people don't get some break in the content, they will not gain as much. Make sessions informative and efficient. Use as little time as you can to get your points across.

Fundraiser

Fundraisers may be a major means to making your organization successful in its goals. There are many types of fundraisers. You can provide a service (car wash), sell items (bake sale, yard sale, candy bars, candles), hold a silent auction (getting items donated), have a dinner (charging more than the amount of the food), or any number of other options.

Things to keep in mind:

❋ Be up front about how the money raised will be spent.

❋ Use the money for what you planned.

❋ Always send "Thank You" notes to those who helped you (those who donated items or services).

❋ When displaying items to sell or for auction- think 'design.' Something that looks clean and organized will bring in more money.

❋ Be excited about your cause but not pushy about the fundraiser.

Event Series

This can be a week of events (Homecoming, Greek Week), a month of events (Black History Month), or events that occur at regular intervals (theme movies, workshop/speaker series). Whatever the case may be, you will end up with many events, over a period of time, that have a central or common element or theme. You will end up planning each event somewhat individually; however, be sure to step back and consider the series as a whole. What is your overall goal or goals and how best can it/they be reached?

Hopefully you now have an understanding of the types of events and which one or ones you will want to put on. Keeping that in mind, we will now look at some common elements for most events. Remember that each event is different and you will learn something every time you do one.

Budget

Every event starts with a budget. It's okay if it's not much; you can have an awesome function on a rather low budget! Just be honest with yourself about it and stick to it. Your first step in the finance department is to talk to your advisor about the school's rules on purchasing. Second, make a list of everything that will cost money and add up how much it will be. This may sound like a no-brainer, but you would be surprised how many times students just assume they will have enough money and start spending right away.

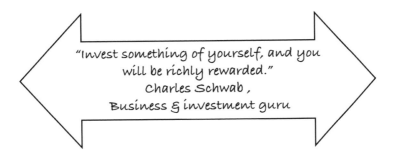

"Invest something of yourself, and you will be richly rewarded."
Charles Schwab,
Business & investment guru

Be sure that you call a couple of places for prices on everything. Some may have competitive pricing, while others may be way off base. Once you have your budget, with estimated prices (facilities, food, etc.), you can really begin to have some fun. If you don't feel your budget is large enough to cover the costs of the event, talk to your advisor or supervisor and ask him or her for more. You may not get it, but it's worth asking. You can also consider holding a fundraiser.

Audience

Before making any major decisions, you will want to assess your audience. Really, there are two major areas here:

1. How many people?
2. Who are they?

The first question may not have an exact answer; however, you will plan differently if you know you are planning for ten people, versus fifty people, versus a couple of hundred people. By "who," I mean, are they students, teachers, members of the community, parents or a combination of everyone? It also includes what type of people they are. What do they like, dislike, etc.? The more specific your answers to these questions, the easier the rest of the planning will be. Always remember that your audience is the most important part of the event. You want to be sure that they are comfortable and have a good time.

> "True leadership must be for
> the benefit of the followers,
> not the enrichment of the leaders."
> Robert Townsend (1920-1998),
> Business executive

"Think ahead. Don't let day-to-day
operations drive out planning."
Donald Rumsfeld,
Former Secretary of Defense

Date

When selecting a date for your event, your best bet is to select your ideal date, then choose a couple of alternate dates (just in case the facilities aren't available, etc.). Selecting these dates can be tricky; and, in fact, perhaps the most difficult part of the planning process. Be sure to look at school and community calendars to see what else is going on around the time you want to have your event.

A few pointers:

✻ Avoid planning events too close to holidays or school breaks (right before or right after)- unless it's a holiday event of course. People generally leave (if not physically, at least mentally) a couple of days before the holiday or break. Also, when they come back from a holiday or break, they will need time to get back in the swing of things and be reminded of the event.

✻ Check all major calendars, including sports calendars. Anything that might compete with drawing in your audience deserves some research.

✻ Select your dates early and be sure they get on calendars. Why not be the event that other groups plan around, instead of trying to plan around everyone else?

Facilities

Where you have your function is important for so many reasons. First of all, the overall feeling of the event will start to be created as soon as people know where you are having it. For example: Outdoor events generally imply a casual atmosphere. Having it at a nice restaurant, community center, or ballroom implies a fancier event. You will want to reserve your facilities as soon as possible. For large, end-of-the-school-year events, it's not a bad idea to start during the first month or so of school.

If you are not sure how many people will be there, or if you have a couple of places you may want to choose from, most places will let you put a "hold" on the facility for a short time. It will probably give you enough time to weigh your options. Wherever you decide to have your event, be sure to check it out in person before you commit to it. Ask how much it will be (total) and when they expect payment. You should check with your advisor to be sure you can fulfill this agreement and to find out who, at your school, needs to sign the contract.

Hint: Never sign a contract for a school until you know the proper procedures. You are not a legal agent for the school and technically can be held personally responsible for what you sign, if you do not go through the school first.

"I would rather have a good plan today than a perfect plan two weeks from now."
General George S. Patton (1885-1945), World War II General

Catering

Depending on what type of event you are having, you may or may not want to serve food. People love food and anytime you provide anything they can eat or drink, they appreciate it. Before committing to a caterer, check around for prices and availability. When you do find the right caterer, tell him or her about the event and what your budget is. Ask what he or she suggests. They may give you a menu or a list of options. Again, be sure to consider your audience. What will they want to eat?

The caterer will want to know how many people will be attending your event. Give your best guess at the moment; you can call in final numbers closer to the date if you need to do so. Caterers know that people do show up last minute, so they will generally set over the amount requested (free of charge), to be sure that no one goes hungry. The average is 10-15% over what you ordered. Be sure to ask what your caterer does, but always give them the actual number you are expecting. You will want to book the caterer as soon as you book the facility. If this event will be held on campus, you should always check on the catering rules of the university before you book anyone. Often schools have a contract with a particular campus food provider. Part of that contract includes not allowing food from other sources in certain buildings.

When deciding on food, here are some things to keep in mind: The time of year the event takes place (Thanksgiving dinners are not what people want in April). Not everyone likes sweets or can eat sweets– for receptions consider a veggie or cheese platter in addition to cookies and cake. Not everyone eats red meat, pork, etc. If you are having a sit-down dinner, be sure to ask guests about dietary restrictions or serve something pretty safe. Be aware of allergies: nuts, gluten, etc. Also, people love choices. If you are serving dessert, offer a couple of different kinds (alternate around the table).

Programming

What will go on at the function? This is a great job for a separate committee that knows the overall intentions of the function. No matter what the event and the program, it is wise to have an agenda. The agenda should account for everything you're planning to do. What time will people begin to arrive? What time will you eat? Do you have a speaker? At what point will he or she be speaking? Who will introduce him or her? Will you have breaks? Remember your audience. The older people get, the less they are able to sit for long periods without a break (your joints get stiff if you are still too long).

If your agenda includes a speaker, disc jockey or band, talk to these people as soon as you have reserved the facilities and have the date of the event. If you are hiring someone from the outside, you will more than likely have a contract to negotiate. Do NOT sign the contract until you check with your advisor about the rules and regulations of contracts. You can, however, do the initial negotiating.

> "Without goals, and plans to reach them, you are like a ship that has set sail with no destination."
> Fitzhugh Dodson (1923-1993), Psychologist, lecturer & writer

Be sure you talk to your performers about: How much money you have for performers and their equipment...total, whether or not you can pay for or provide certain things (such as food– in some cases you may not be able to pay for food, depending on the funding source), and exactly what you want them to do/accomplish. If you're bringing in a speaker, let them know if you have specific things you wish them to address. If you are bringing in a disc jockey, be sure you have let him or her know what you expect and what the school does not allow. Performer needs should be listed in the Rider. A Contract Rider is a document in which the performers list all of their needs and wants. It might include a request for hotel accommodations and/or green M&Ms. They can pretty much put anything in the document, but it is up to you and your school to decide what you will, or even can, do. I have even seen some riders in which the performers requested certain alcohol be provided in their trailers or rooms. Be sure you read everything through and have your advisor do the same. Once the contract is signed, you are legally bound to it.

Decorations

Where you have your function and what type of function it is will help you decide what to do about decorations, as well as your budget. Check out discount stores, party stores, and don't forget online party suppliers– many times they are cheaper than you could ever imagine. Decorations set the mood once people are there. Before you buy anything, think about what you want the overall feeling of the event to be. This is another great area for a separate committee. A bit of advice: Be sure you are all on the same page, before you begin. Sketch out what everything will look like. Also, be sure you schedule people you know are reliable to help you put up the decorations. You will more than likely be putting them up the day of the actual event. If people don't show up, you may not finish in enough time to do what you need to do before the event begins.

Invitations

"Hard work spotlights the character of people: some turn up their sleeves, some turn up their noses, and some don't turn up at all…"
Sam Ewing, Athlete

Whether you are sending out formal invitations, posting flyers, putting an ad in the paper, using social media or any combination thereof, you will want to be sure people know about the event well in advance. If you want people to respond (RSVP- French phrase, Respondez, s'il vous plait or Please Respond), send out the invitations three to five weeks in advance and ask for the RSVP about a week and a half to two weeks before the event – allowing some time for them to come in. Be aware that some who have RSVP'd will not show up and some that did not RSVP will show up. They usually end up about the same number, canceling each other out– so don't stress about it; just expect it. A week before the event, call the caterer with the numbers you have. When to send the invitation will depend on how big of an event it is. How large your budget is will be a good indicator. The larger the budget, the earlier the notification, but no earlier than five weeks or people may forget about the event. You may send out a "Save the Date" notification anytime you wish, so people can plan early to attend.

An invitation should explain what the event is, why it is happening, how people should dress, etc. If you are having a meal, you will want to have a space on your RSVP card to address dietary restrictions and needs, as well as a place to indicate if your guest will be bringing another guest. Continuing with the formal dinner theme here, if you are doing place cards (to let everyone know where they are sitting), be sure to consider all the people you are putting at a particular table. Do they get along? If they don't know each other, do they have enough in common to strike up a conversation? Another way to designate seating (without actual place cards) is table numbers. Assign each table with a number, putting the number somewhere at the table itself, and let guests know which table they will be sitting at when they check in.

> "Doing your best at this moment puts
> you in the best place
> for the next moment."
> Oprah Winfrey,
> TV host, producer & philanthropist

Dress code:

❋ Formal/Black Tie = tuxedo or gown

❋ Black Tie Optional = tuxedo or gown OR suit (with tie) or evening/cocktail dress (Couples should match. If the lady is wearing a gown, the gentleman should wear a tuxedo. If the gentleman is wearing a suit, the lady should wear an evening/cocktail dress.)

❋ Business Attire = suits

❋ Business Casual = slacks and a nice shirt for men, slacks/skirt and blouse or dress for the ladies.

❋ Casual = depending on the event, this could be "business casual" or blue jeans.

Marketing

Common Marketing Methods

🌼 *Press Releases*. This is an article you write and send to the media alerting them of the information. Be sure to include information about the event (who, what, when, where, why, etc.) and your contact information, in case they have more questions. Keep these brief and to the point.

> "If you see a snake, just kill it. Don't appoint a committee on snakes."
> H. Ross Perot,
> Businessman &
> former US Presidential candidate

🌼 *Posters, flyers, handbills (mini flyers), table tents, etc.* When doing a flyer, don't put it up too early. If selling tickets, give people about a month. If the event is free, about a week and a half to two weeks is perfect. If your flyer, poster, table tent, or ad in the paper is put out there too early, people may think, "I want to go to that." But with such busy lives, they forget about it before it gets here. Remember, some people make plans weeks ahead; others are rather last minute. You want to find a compromise and try to reach both audiences.

🌼 *Word of Mouth*. Never underestimate this! It is a powerful tool. Spread the word in class, in other organizations... tell your friends to do the same.

🌼 *Promotional Items*. Finding just the right promotional item can really get the word out about your event and will also promote your organization well. A coffee mug, for example, promoting your Coffee House Concert is perfect.

🌼 *Alternative Marketing*. May include dressing up in costumes to make announcements at key times, playing the music of a band that is coming, and anything else that is creative and will attract attention to your event.

❀ ***Unique 2U***- Facebook, Twitter, and other online communities can be amazing tools for marketing. Creating an event and inviting everyone you know (or your target audience, at least) can seal the deal on attendance to your event. You can also start groups for the committees. If you want, you can even take out a banner ad for your school or region… it is a very cost effective way to reach a lot of people.

Common marketing mistakes

❀ Getting the word out too late. The day before is *too late*– often, so is the week of– shoot for at least two weeks out.

❀ Forgetting to include important information (Date, time, location, sponsoring organization, etc.)

❀ Putting too much on a poster (If it looks confusing or has too much text, people will simply not read it.)

❀ Not using your resources (Asking the school paper to do an article is a great idea– also, ask teacher/professors if you can make an announcement at the end of class, particularly if it is relevant to the class.)

❀ Expecting that the same strategies work for every event (Think about who you are trying to reach… how can you best reach *them*?).

❀ Using only one form of marketing (Just social media or flyers, etc.)

❀ Skimping on the marketing budget (Often people think that since it is not the actual event, they can reduce the budget here. The reality is that if people don't know about the event, it doesn't really matter how great it is. Try to shoot for about 10% of your budget going to marketing.)

Run Through

This does not necessarily mean you have to act out everything. About a month before the event, get together as a group and go over the event together– every item on the agenda. Ask yourselves what will happen and what *could* happen for each item. Plan for any problems that may arise. I have done this with camps, banquets, weddings, concerts, campus-wide events, BINGO nights– you name it. You will be amazed at what you come up with sometimes. Other times, you may realize that everything is ready to go. Don't skip this step. It doesn't take much time and can really save you trouble and potential embarrassment.

Record Keeping and Evaluations

Keep a record of everyone you talk to, what they said and what you said; keep a record of everything you did and decided to do. This will help if you need to call someone back, if there is a problem or someone doesn't do what they said they would do. Plus, it will help with planning the next event. You may think you will remember the conversations, but keep in mind you are also taking classes and have other things going on.

When you are finished with the event, call a meeting with everyone who helped plan the event. Ask what worked, what did not work and decide what you will do/change for the next event. This meeting should be an honest discussion. Your goal is to figure out how to make the event the best it can be. Even if you are not planning to do the event again, it is still a good idea to evaluate it. You will learn some things to do and to avoid for other events you may do in the future.

IN THE END

The journey you are on is not the easiest. Finding out what your strengths are, what you are meant to do and who you are meant to be, can all be very frustrating at times. But I promise you, no one is going to be better at it than you. There is a place in this world that is empty without you. It is just waiting for you to make your choices and then, show up.

I have known far too many people who put off doing what they believed in and becoming the person they wanted to be for so long, that life eventually made other choices for them. It is funny how it all works... You get a chance to make your life choices. If you don't make them, someone else will do it for you. And believe me, if you don't like it, it is much more difficult (though not impossible) to change your situation, the older you get. So, do what you need to do now, while you have the opportunity. Whether you are able to see it or not, you do have choices and support is out there.

I wish that I could honestly tell you that this journey out of high school and through college will be your toughest, but unfortunately, that is unlikely to be the case. You will be faced with challenges, heartaches, fears, physical ailments, and a host of other unpleasant feelings and occurrences throughout your whole life. It is not always as depressing as all that though. You will also be presented with joys beyond your imagination, love, wonder, promotions, and dreams coming true. Hopefully, your joys will outweigh your sorrows.